SOLDIER OF FINANCE

SOLDIER OF
FINANCE

TAKE CHARGE OF YOUR MONEY AND INVEST IN YOUR FUTURE

JEFF ROSE, CFP®

AMACOM

American Management Association

New York • Atlanta • Brussels • Chicago • Mexico City • San Francisco
Shanghai • Tokyo • Toronto • Washington, D.C.

This publication is designed to provide accurate and authoritative information in regard to the subject matter covered. It is sold with the understanding that the publisher is not engaged in rendering legal, accounting, or other professional service. If legal advice or other expert assistance is required, the services of a competent professional person should be sought.

Library of Congress Cataloging-in-Publication Data

Rose, Jeff (Business writer)
   Soldier of finance : take charge of your money and invest in your future / Jeff Rose.
      pages cm
   Includes index.
   ISBN 978-0-8144-3328-7 (pbk.) — ISBN 0-8144-3328-6 (pbk.) 1. Finance, Personal.
2. Investments. I. Title.
   HG179.R647 2013
   332.024--dc23   2013007813

ABOUT AMA

American Management Association (www.amanet.org) is a world leader in talent development, advancing the skills of individuals to drive business success. Our mission is to support the goals of individuals and organizations through a complete range of products and services, including classroom and virtual seminars, webcasts, webinars, podcasts, conferences, corporate and government solutions, business books, and research. AMA's approach to improving performance combines experiential learning—learning through doing—with opportunities for ongoing professional growth at every step of one's career journey.

Printing number
10 9 8 7 6 5 4 3 2 1

DEDICATION

To my wife, **Mandy**, who supports and inspires me in
everything I do. Without your constant encouragement this
book would continue to be just another "big idea."

To my three boys, **Parker**, **Bentley**, and **Sloane**, who give
me the drive to be a better father, provider, and leader.

To all our **U.S. military service men and women**
who continue to fight for our freedom.

In memory of **SSG Joshua Melton**, a true American hero
who volunteered to defend the country he loved
so that his wife, daughter, and future generations
would always know freedom.

The test of success is not what you do when you are on top.
Success is how high you bounce when you hit bottom.
—GEORGE S. PATTON

CONTENTS

ACKNOWLEDGMENTS

My dad used to tell me that if I continued to dream big, big things would come. Several years ago I dreamed about writing and publishing a book. What you are holding in your hands is the product of never letting others squash that dream.

First and foremost, I want to thank Jesus Christ my lord and savior. Your ability to constantly provide, forgive, and always be present in my life helps me to be a better man every day.

If you Google "super awesome wife," the number-one result should be my wife Mandy. She listens to every single "Big Idea" that I have, which is basically an everyday occurrence. She calmly takes them in stride, making her an easy candidate for wife of the year.

Her ability to run a household with three rambunctious boys—love you Parker, Bentley, and Sloane!—while I worked on getting this book done many a late night is just one of the many reasons why I know that I found my soul mate.

The U.S. Army National Guard took a nineteen-year-old lost soul and turned him into a man with a purpose. The discipline and drive that I gained through my training is immeasurable. For that, I offer an exultant "Hoooah!"

When I was a child, my father spoiled me with every G.I. Joe and Transformer I could ever hope for. Despite all the toys, it was fatherly love and willingness to just listen that will always mean the world to me. He never doubted my success as I never doubted how much he loved me. Miss you, Pops!

My mother sports the same stubbornness as I, but even though she was just 4'11", I knew better than to mess with a stern Filipino woman. In fact, I feared her more than some of my drill sergeants in basic training! She might not get all the big plans that her son is up to, but she's constantly proud to talk me up to her friends and family. That's all that a son could ask for.

Over a dozen publishing houses told me "no" before AMACOM said "yes." Thank you for taking a chance on a first-time author.

So many others had a dramatic impact in my life and making this book possible. I owe you all my sincerest love and gratitude: Rick and Jeanie Wilson (the best in-laws a son could have), Ben Newman, Matt Sapaula, Steve Ross, Don Enevoldsen, Les O'Dell, Mike Stephens, Phil Tirone, The Strategic Coaching Program, Adrienne Duffy, Ryan Guina, Phil Taylor, Monte Kuhnert (for hiring a kid straight out of college to be your junior broker), Common Grounds Coffee House, Adam Baker, and the Financial Blogging Community.

INTRODUCTION

"What the hell am I doing here?"

Those were not the words I wanted on my mind. But they forced themselves on me anyway. A drill sergeant boomed over my head, "Seven, six, five . . . " counting down from ten for the third time. Each time he reached zero, I did more push-ups. My hands were already shaking, without the extra work.

Ten more push-ups and he gave up on me. "Get the f--- out of my face and get to formation."

Anyone who has ever tried something new has experienced those moments of wondering whether it was all a serious mistake. That was my moment. I had just joined the U.S. Army. We weren't even to Basic Training yet, and already I felt like I was in over my head. This was Reception, where we waited for our call-up to Basic, or as we called it, "Down Range."

About all we did to fill our days was one formation after another. It seemed like every hour, with little warning, an order would come to fall in and to wear a particular uniform. It might be, "Formation's gonna be in BDUs," which is military for battle dress uniform. Or the order specified that we wear gloves, or make sure we had our hats. Everyone had to look exactly the same.

That particular hour, the order was for winter PTs. That's military for cold weather physical training outfits. I was ready to go except for my jacket, which was stuffed safely in my duffel bag, securely padlocked underneath my bunk.

The problem was, the dial on the combination lock faced away from me. To see it, I had to get on my back on the floor, peering under the bunk. Making matters worse, I hadn't memorized the combination yet. It was on a sticker in my neck wallet, which my shaking hands could not pull out fast enough.

The drill sergeant decided to help motivate me. "Private, you've got ten seconds before I put my foot . . . " I won't finish the sentence. You can probably guess.

I never had any hope of getting that bag open. After three attempts, and three sets of push-ups, I headed to formation without my jacket. Although I was afraid that I would get special attention in the formation since I was the only one who looked different, I somehow escaped without further harassment.

And I got through the training. Each stressful situation increased my understanding and ability to deal with a wide variety of situations. I discovered one step at a time that I could do it, that I could do almost anything if I wanted to and if I prepared properly. As uncomfortable as some of those situations were, the training was invaluable.

THE *SOLDIER'S* HANDBOOK

At Reception, we began our military training and took on the appearance of soldiers. Substance would come later.

Here we filled out the final paperwork, lined up for the painful indignity of a series of shots, and received our first military haircut, the stylish bald look.

Moving on to collect our gear, we were supplied two duffel bags and a rucksack filled to the brim with every essential item necessary

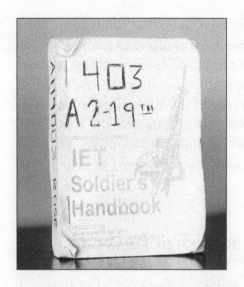

for the following three months and beyond. Among the collection of standard-issue items were glasses—aptly called BCGs, or "Birth Control Glasses," a perfect complement to the bald look—a canteen, boots, uniform, and a flashlight.

Buried there in the carefully organized muddle was a small paperback book: the *IET Soldier's Handbook*. IET is military for Initial Entry Training.

The most important things in life are often the most mundane in appearance. This book, about the size of a brick, was intended, like the masonry product, to give us a firm foundation upon which to build careers of service to the United States.

The *Soldier's Handbook* didn't look like much, but we soon discovered it was the single most important piece of equipment issued that day. Every new recruit was required to carry it at all times. If one of our drill sergeants caught us without it, the consequences were not pretty or pleasant. The handbook was our survival guide, our operation manual, our answer book. And our training blueprint. Everything we needed to learn to function in military life was laid out in its 258 pages.

The purpose of the *IET Soldier's Handbook* was to navigate us through obstacles and provide the basic knowledge necessary to become efficient soldiers. Its single purpose was to prepare us to conquer the enemy.

That book, now tattered and looking as though it went through a war (perhaps because it did), sits on my desk, a constant reminder that I survived a tour of duty in a war zone and not only survived, but functioned at a high level of effectiveness, in large part because

I was prepared. You can't predict everything that will happen, but I knew what resources and weapons were available to me and how to use them. I knew what to expect from the enemy and how to turn every attack to advantage. It inspired me to always be ready, and to take advantage of every opportunity. In short, it trained me to win.

This book still serves me today, many years after the conclusion of my military career. It continues to inspire and motivate me. It also became the initial seed for the book you are holding in your hands.

THE PURPOSE OF *SOLDIER OF FINANCE*

You don't have to be a soldier to benefit from *Soldier of Finance*. I share my military experience primarily because the principles I learned for surviving combat and winning against an enemy on the battlefield are the same principles I needed to survive financial problems, enabling me to engineer a winning strategy for building stable and enduring wealth.

Most people I meet, especially those who come to me for financial counsel, struggle with finances. They exist in a kind of war zone where debt is the enemy and wealth is the goal. But they have a tough time getting a handle on their own money and they worry over their future security. Most are losing a battle they don't even consciously realize they are in. I have found that there are two basic problems common to the majority of those I talk with:

1. Lack of information

2. Lack of initiative

By approaching my own finances with the mindset I learned in the military, I found the resources and the attitude that I needed to get myself out of debt and begin a successful program of investment. Even if you've never been in the military, you will find within the pages of this book the information needed to build financial security and growth.

If you find yourself asking, as I did my first day at Reception, "What the hell am I doing here?" the answer is simple. You are training yourself to win. You are gaining the essential knowledge and discipline to be a Soldier of Finance.

This manual is organized in modular format so that you can easily identify the areas of greatest benefit to you. I recommend that you read the entire book first, in order to find the areas where you need the most help. Then use it as a reference guide for future planning. You'll find that each section deals with an essential part of your financial success.

The two chapters of Part One tell something of my own story, providing encouragement to those who believe they have no hope because they've made mistakes. I made plenty too, and I've done pretty well.

Part Two addresses the Initial Training Phase of becoming a Soldier of Finance, covering the basics of getting your financial life under control. If you are already in a mess, the goal is to stop the bleeding. You can achieve this by exploring the basics of credit: how to find your credit score, check your credit record, and learn what can be done to fix bad credit. Demonstrating how to set realistic goals and prioritize objectives, Part Two explores methods to keep yourself on track and discover ways to convert your debt into a positive cash flow.

Part Three is the Campaign Phase, designed to familiarize you with the tools available for turning your resources into long-term wealth. It covers the basics of budgeting and explains a variety of investment vehicles.

Part Four, the Consolidation Phase, discusses the last stages of accomplishing your mission, including real estate investing and the types of insurance you need to protect yourself from the unexpected.

Each chapter contains a Go/No Go test. These evaluations are designed to help you gauge your progress. Take the time to fill out each one as you come to it. It will help you identify areas that need work and give you the information you need to prepare your strategy.

The battle is not as difficult as you might think, provided you have the right information and training. In spite of recent economic troubles, opportunity is everywhere. The problem is fear of the unknown. Few people know what to expect from the enemy or what weapons are at their disposal; for lack of knowledge, they struggle and suffer. Unsure of what to do, they either do nothing or make decisions that create more problems than they solve.

As I write this, the U.S. Census Bureau reports that Americans are battling more than $2.9 trillion in consumer debt, unemployment is at record highs, millions of dollars have been lost from 401(k) accounts, and more than half of all Americans have no money saved for retirement. Absolutely none.

The solution? Prepare for the battle. Basic was not easy and there were times I questioned whether or not I could make it, but when I found myself in combat, I knew what to do and how to do it because I was well prepared. The key to success is action based on knowledge.

This is your *Soldier of Finance Handbook*. It covers the basics you must understand in order to evaluate the enemy, set up your plan of attack, and not only survive financial difficulties, but *conquer* them efficiently and effectively. No matter where you are now or how hopeless your finances might seem, you are about to turn things around. Welcome to Basic.

DISCOVERY PHASE: WHAT IS YOUR WHY?

Part One is designed to help you take a deep look inside yourself. Before you can make any improvements to your current situation, you have to understand what got you there in the first place. This will require that you confront some tough personal issues about your past financial choices, so be prepared.

By the end of the Discovery Phase you'll have a better understanding of what makes you tick and how we can address that together.

WHY ARE YOU HERE?

"Why?" That is the first question you must ask yourself.

Why are you here? Why are you struggling with finances? Why haven't you been more successful? Why are you reading this book?

As straightforward as those questions appear, you will find that getting to the real root of your current situation in life requires honest reflection. For example, to simply claim that you are struggling because your job doesn't pay you enough is not getting to the heart of the problem. The real issue is much deeper. If your job doesn't pay enough, what are you doing to improve your situation? Complaining or feeling sorry for yourself will not get you anywhere.

For most people, there are two reasons for not making changes. One is that they don't know what to do. Presumably, the fact that you are reading this indicates that you are willing to try to fix that problem.

The second reason is more difficult: intimidation, or fear of the unknown. If you are not familiar with the world of finance, the terminology can be imposing. It's hard to try a new direction when nothing in your experience enables you to predict the outcome.

The question "Why?" is a useful tool in overcoming those obstacles. Before doing anything, you need to figure out what is holding you back, what habit patterns and thought processes keep you where you are. And equally important, what will push you enough to make a change?

Ask yourself some questions. What motivates you? Why do you want to get out of debt? What makes you want to take control of your financial life? What stirs enough passion in you to take action?

To find these answers, you will need to look back at the defining moments in your life, the ones that made you who you are today. I had to face the very questions that you have to ask yourself. And to answer them, I had to concede that some of my early perceptions of life were wrong.

When I was young, my dad was my hero, my Superman. As a kid, I believed he could do no wrong. He was a great father, and I wanted very much to be like him. But as I got older, I started to see some problems. I realized he did not manage his finances well. In fact, he was the epitome of what you shouldn't do. He struggled to pay bills. Every month he worried about where the money would come from. The reason became clear when I began to analyze his financial habits: Racking up credit card debt at an alarming rate, he used cash advance loans on one credit card to make the minimum payment on another one. He had a second mortgage and he repeatedly had his house reappraised so he could borrow more against it.

As I got older, I knew that I didn't want to struggle every month like my father. I did not want credit card debt. Nor did I want to worry all the time. I wanted nothing to do with those problems. Ultimately, that desire was strong enough to motivate me to change.

I'm not saying I did everything right the first time around. I screwed up almost from the beginning. Nearly everyone does. I share my own journey to encourage the understanding that you can make progress in your own life, even if you've managed to create serious damage from the start.

SHAKY BEGINNINGS

My dad was a very no-nonsense guy. He never attended college. Instead, he joined the 101st Airborne and served for two years. After the Army, he bounced around several odd jobs before realizing that not having a college degree hurt his ability to obtain a respectable, well-paying career. At the age of 55 he returned to school and finally got his degree.

The life lesson he sought to ingrain in me was to *not* follow in his footsteps: Go to school and get a degree. He adamantly wanted me to avoid the regrets that plagued him. I had every intention of following his advice. Fresh out of high school, my sights were set on a business career, not the military. I had a plan, simple and straightforward—I would enroll in community college, move on to a four-year degree, graduate, and begin my successful life as an adult. It sounded perfect and attainable. What could go wrong?

The problem was that I really wasn't quite prepared to be an adult. I didn't think the whole thing through very well. Failing to set clear goals, I didn't pursue my education with the persistence or forethought necessary for success. A series of obstacles proved too much for my aspirations.

In retrospect, some of my problems were glaringly obvious. To begin with, I relied on my mom to help me out. Without her financial support, I couldn't even get into college. She and my dad had been separated for several years, so I depended on her to take responsibility for my life. She was paying the bills, and I anticipated that would include college—not exactly an adult way to start. To her credit, she started the process of pushing me out of the nest. She expected me to do something. Instead of mailing a check to the college, she handed me her credit card and sent me off to the campus to make my first tuition payment.

We lived in Southern California at the time, in the San Fernando Valley. The school I chose to begin my adult journey was Santa Monica Community College. I confidently stepped into the registration office, borrowed credit card in hand. That's when I learned the first lesson of business. Pay attention to details. Those you do business with most likely will.

The woman behind the counter took the card, looked at it, looked at me, looked back at the card, and looked at me again. Then she spoke. "You don't look like *Lilly*."

They wouldn't accept the card. I had no cash, no checkbook, and no way to pay.

Santa Monica Community College was a short 18-mile drive from my home down the 405 freeway. That sounds simple enough, but anyone who has ever lived in the Los Angeles area knows that the 405 often looks more like a parking lot than a major highway. I wasn't anxious to make the trip home, back to Santa Monica, and home again in one day. That short 18 miles could easily take three hours.

"Fine," I said. "I'll come back later." Later turned into several days. That's when I learned my second lesson about being an adult: If you want to succeed you have to take responsibility for your choices, and you must live with the consequences when you don't. I walked back into the registration office several days later, check in hand, ready to start my adult journey, but the woman at the counter shook her head.

"The deadline for tuition payments was three days ago. You've been dropped from all your classes."

I would have liked to blame my mom for sending me off with a form of payment that she should have known wouldn't be accepted. I could have blamed the registration person, who neglected to tell me that the deadline was approaching. And I could have blamed it on Southern California traffic engineers, who ought to have designed a more efficient and less intimidating freeway system. Blame shifting, however, is a sign of immaturity, and will never lead you to success.

I screwed up. I had to admit it to myself and take the steps to correct the problem. Gathering the information I needed to proceed, I asked, "What do I have to do to get back into my classes?"

"First, you have to take the responsibility to go to each class instructor." At that point, I didn't really *like* that word, "responsibility," very much. But it wouldn't go away. Once I contacted each instructor, I essentially had to beg to get back into that class and hope the instructor would approve. I've never liked begging, but there was no alternative.

Making the 18-mile drive again, I tracked down two instructors, both of whom gave me the same story. The classes had filled and there were no slots available. There was nothing they could do.

Discouraged, I did what any not-quite-adult-yet person would do. I moped back to my car. Tucked unobtrusively under the windshield wiper was a parking ticket for $75. That was the last straw. I quit. Apparently it wasn't meant to be. Not for that semester, maybe not ever.

Decisions have consequences, and consequences are often painful. I now had to tell my family. I wasn't worried about my mom; she had learned to let me be me. The call I dreaded was to my father, who I knew would be terribly disappointed.

Nervously pacing back and forth, I dialed his number, putting my deodorant to the test. I hoped he would be too busy to answer. Unfortunately, he answered on the first ring. I eased into the conversation. "Hey Dad! How are things?" We exchanged the usual pleasantries. Finding no easy segue to what I needed to say, I finally blurted it out. "Dad, I got dropped from my classes and I'm taking the semester off."

Silence.

A little bit of yelling would have been easier to take. His disappointment was palpable. He wanted me to avoid his failures, and I was letting the opportunity slip away from me.

I tried to reassure him that it was only temporary. I would only take off one semester, just a few months. He understood the reality, though. One semester turns into two, and two into a lifetime. He had already been down that road.

Reminding me how much he regretted waiting all of those years to get his college education, he calculated what the delay cost him, and affirmed that he wanted better for me.

That gentle exhortation was the extent of my dad's comments. He could have been as harsh as I feared he might be, but that wasn't my dad. He remained even-keeled in spite of his disappointment.

During the next few months I never got close to a classroom. Instead, I moved into a cubicle. My mom convinced her boss to give me a temporary full-time position. She was an account manager at Applause Inc., a company that made stuffed animals. Monday through Friday, eight hours a day, I sat in my tiny cell, entering data. It didn't take long to realize this was not what I wanted to do with my life. I began to truly regret missing the tuition deadline.

My unhappiness started to affect every aspect of my life. Butting heads with my mom, I avoided her whenever I could and stayed isolated in my room, jamming out to '90s grunge music whenever I was home. The rest of the time, I worked out at the gym or hung out with friends. I remember that part of my life odiously. Nothing I was doing was getting me to where I wanted to be.

A couple of friends in Illinois where I used to live with my father had joined the Army National Guard. They raved about the benefits, which included the chance to fully fund their college degrees with a six-year obligation of one weekend per month and two weeks in the summer.

The biggest problem with failure is not that we failed, but that we so often let the past dictate our future. Initially, I dismissed the idea. I was not even responsible enough to pay my own tuition on time; how could I possibly take on the responsibility to serve my country?

What motivated me to finally take action was the simple fact that I was so miserable where I was. I looked at my life and I hated what I saw. I had to do something. I was miserable enough that I decided I had nothing to lose. So I picked up the phone and called the recruiter.

Then I called my dad. This time the conversation was different. He would never have encouraged me to join the military, but I know he was pleased with my choice, especially when I told him about the benefits. He was particularly excited to learn that the Army would pay for me to go back to school.

Why do I share this with you? To let you know that I was a screwup. We all make mistakes. I am not suggesting that if you are having financial difficulties, you need to join the Army. I joined, and I'm sharing my lessons so you can learn without taking several years out of your life. Don't worry about finding your local recruiter's number! By applying the lessons I have learned, you will be able to take responsibility for your life, and regain control.

Understand that nothing you've done in the past can prevent you from succeeding now, if you are willing to make changes and take the initiative to do something positive. I made many mistakes along the way. I never needed to join the Army. In many ways, it was an unnecessary detour. But while I was there, I gained valuable experience that I use today and will continue to benefit from for the rest of my life. Instead of letting your past hold you back, learn to let it drive you. Determine why you want to succeed, and allow that knowledge to sustain you when things are rough.

WHAT'S YOUR STORY?

As a financial advisor, I encounter people daily in a state of financial ruin who are unwilling to accept the fact they are the culprits. It's always someone else's fault—the economy, the president, their family, or their heritage. I'm sure you know people like this. Perhaps it describes you. If so, until you stop blaming others and take responsibility for your own life, you will never make progress. Know that you are not alone. Many people struggle with finances:

- $3,800: average American's savings account balance

- 40%: percentage of Americans who are *not* saving for retirement

- 25%: percentage of Americans who have nothing saved for retirement

- $117,951: average American household debt

It doesn't have to be that way. I realized that there was something better for me than the eight-to-five cubicle life, and I made a choice that changed my future. I became a Soldier of Finance.

WHAT IS A SOLDIER OF FINANCE?

You too have a choice. You don't have to join the military to change your life, but the analogy of being in the Army might help you determine the choices you need to make. The obstacles that stand in the way of success are enemies to your future. To overcome them, follow the approach a soldier takes when he goes into combat:

- Learn discipline.

- Train yourself to deal with the financial situations you will face.

- Plan a campaign to systematically learn how finances work and then implement those lessons to achieve your goals.

Soldiers of Finance are people who commit to whatever it takes to change the direction of their lives and overcome whatever is preventing success, thus building security for themselves and their families. If any of those goals describe *you*, then *you* are a perfect candidate to become a Soldier of Finance.

DEBRIEFING

A Soldier of Finance Success Story

A Soldier of Finance has to always be alert and recognize that the enemy could be all around at any time. If the enemy is engaged in a full-fledged assault, you may have to take drastic measures. At the age of 25, Adam Baker found himself on what he called the "typical American life path." He was—in his words—*"doing just fine."* He had a start-up real estate business and a girlfriend who was finishing college to become a teacher. She also was *"doing just fine."* Adam tells their story:

"Now, years later, I understand the 'just fine' was code for 'I haven't missed a payment.' We had each found a way to juggle our ever-increasing monthly payments on our limited incomes. For us, that was just fine.

The 18 months that followed were . . . interesting. Courtney accepted my proposal; we married within the year, and pregnancy came knocking a few months after the wedding.

Dazed, married, and pregnant, we had come down with a hardcore case of house fever, car fever, and just about any other consumerist fever you can imagine.

We had managed to collect two car loans, several credit cards, a line of credit at the jewelry store, a loan from parents, and more than $50,000 in student loans. The total damage was just over $80,000 in non-mortgage debt throughout the various loans. We knew the next step well: buy a house and fill it in with a bunch of crap. And yes, we were looking.

Luckily, a life event jolted our system and made us reevaluate our priorities. A month after celebrating our first anniversary, our daughter Milligan was born. During the pregnancy we began to give our financial situation a closer look, but things didn't really sink in until we brought her home.

Looking back, I guess we were willing to be risky when it was just the two of us. We were willing to bet on our success down the road to pick up the bill of our lifestyle desires now. Fortunately, we realized we weren't willing to wager Milligan's future.

We finally came to terms with how limiting our debt made our lives, how much it weighed on our freedom. We made the decision right then and there to take back control over our life.

At first, we struggled with the basics of budgeting, tracking spending, and curbing our impulses. But we quickly found that the more we simplified our financial life, the more empowered we became."

GO/NO GO

Are you ready to get started? One of the responsibilities of a sergeant is to check efficiency on basic skills, what we called Warrior Skills or Common Training Tasks, which include everything from evaluating a casualty to performing maintenance on a vehicle. These skills are considered essential for every soldier to be considered combat ready.

The Go/No Go test that follows has been adapted for a Soldier of Finance. Each chapter contains its own Go/No Go evaluation to check your progress. Be honest as you check the appropriate response for each question.

Go / No Go

Performance Measure

Are all of your bills current? Are you making late payments on anything?

_____ **Go**   _____ **No Go**

Do you regularly use a budget?

_____ **Go**   _____ **No Go**

Do you keep your checkbook balanced?

_____ **Go**   _____ **No Go**

Without looking, do you know how many credit cards you have?

_____ **Go**   _____ **No Go**

(Continues on next page)

If you suddenly had to pay for a $500 car repair or other emergency, could you do it in cash without borrowing?

_____ **Go**   _____ **No Go**

Do you know your credit score?

_____ **Go**   _____ **No Go**

Do you regularly save for retirement in an IRA, 401(k), 403(b), or other plan?

_____ **Go**   _____ **No Go**

Can you explain what a Roth IRA is?

_____ **Go**   _____ **No Go**

If you were to become disabled, could your family survive without your income?

_____ **Go**   _____ **No Go**

If you were to die unexpectedly, would your family be taken care of financially?

_____ **Go**   _____ **No Go**

Do you have health insurance and homeowners (or renters) insurance?

_____ **Go**   _____ **No Go**

Do you have automobile insurance beyond what is required by law?

_____ **Go**   _____ **No Go**

If you scored more *No Go's* than *Go's*, drop and give me twenty push-ups. That won't actually help your finances, but at least you can stop feeling that you deserve some sort of punishment for being a failure. The truth is, your situation is far from hopeless. So get over that emotion and come back to reality. This is not a test. It is an evaluation that demonstrates what needs the most work. If you acknowledged a problem that you have ignored most of your life, then you have made progress and no punishment is required. You now understand some of the tasks we will address in this book.

SUMMARY

- Overcoming financial problems starts with getting to the root of why you are in the position you are in.

- There are two reasons people don't make changes: (1) they don't know what to do, or (2) they are intimidated.

- To change, you need to understand what is holding you back and, just as important, what would motivate you enough to make a change.

- Many people struggle with finances. But it doesn't have to be that way: You have a choice.

- A Soldier of Finance is a person who has become committed to the process of financial discipline and training in order to develop a systematic strategy for financial success.

- Evaluate the areas of personal finance in which you need to work, but don't get discouraged. The situation is not hopeless.

TIME TO ENLIST
AND TAKE AN OATH

I, Jeff Rose, do solemnly swear that I will support and defend the Constitution of the United States against all enemies, foreign and domestic; that I will bear true faith and allegiance to the same; and that I will obey the orders of the President of the United States and the orders of the officers appointed over me, according to regulations and the Uniform Code of Military Justice. So help me God.

So began my official military career. I took an oath.

A couple of preliminaries occurred before that moment; I arrived at MEPS (Military Entrance Processing Station) and was subjected to a thorough medical exam. I'll come back to that experience later. Essentially, the Army had to be sure it actually wanted me. There were a few papers to sign. And I had to be sure I actually wanted the Army. Once everyone was certain that we wanted each other, I was sworn in. "I, Jeff Rose . . . "

It might seem on the surface that this was a frivolous formality. For many people, talk is cheap. It means little in terms of the bigger picture of life. How many times have people said to you, "Let's get together for lunch," and that's the last you hear from them? Or how often have people carelessly told you they would do something that they never got around to?

This oath felt different. Perhaps it was the formality. Perhaps it was the way the military embraces traditions. From the beginning, the oath of enlistment carried great weight in our thinking. We didn't take it lightly, for a couple of reasons.

First of all, we instinctively knew that the day might come when our lives depended on the faithfulness of our buddies to that oath. From that moment, we were all dedicated to the same purpose—serving our country and supporting each other in the process. The implications of commitment were clear and hung over us like a banner.

Second, there's something powerful that happens when you state your commitment clearly, out loud, in front of witnesses. No longer an idea for the future or something you will do one day, the oath becomes a definitive starting point from which you can measure your progress and your success. Your personal honor is engaged and quitting is no longer an easy option. The oath gives you a clean point of transition. Life is about to change.

Becoming a Soldier of Finance requires a similar moment of commitment. You are about to change your life. The financial habits that have caused you difficulty in the past need to change. You are about to embark on a training regimen that will give you the skills and knowledge to replace your old way of handling money to something far more stable and successful.

I encourage you to take this step seriously. Do not just read over it, believing that mental agreement with what you read is enough. Make it formal and make it real. Raise your right hand and read the Soldier of Finance Oath out loud. No one will come after you if you default, other than possibly the IRS and a few credit card companies, but hearing the words come out of your own mouth will help close the door to going back. New training is about to begin and procrastination is no longer acceptable. This oath gives you a clear starting point.

Ask yourself a simple question: *"Am I serious about gaining control of my financial life?"* If the answer is yes, then the time for commitment is now. Raise your hand and repeat after me:

> *I (NAME) do solemnly swear that I will support and defend the principles of the* Soldier of Finance *survival guide; that I will bear true faith and allegiance to the same; and that I will obey the orders of* Soldier of Finance *and the directives presented in the Soldier of Finance doctrine. So help me God.*

In the *Soldier's Handbook*, the Oath of Enlistment is followed by the Soldier's Creed. I found it useful to refer to it from time to time as a reminder of the commitment I had made. The Creed reminded me of things like, "I am an American Soldier," and "I will never quit." It reiterated my training with declarations like, "I am disciplined, physically and mentally tough, trained, and proficient," and "I am an expert and I am a professional."

As a Soldier of Finance, you also have a Creed to help you stay on course, a reminder of why you are learning the lessons of this book. It is a statement of personal values and of your mission in life.

SOLDIER OF FINANCE CREED
I am a Soldier of Finance.
I respect, but do not worship, money.
I control my finances, they do not control me.
I plan my money mission carefully and execute that mission.
Turning my back on fads and status, I focus on what is important.
I am honest, fair, and prepared.
I am ready for future events, both planned and unexpected.
I stand ready to learn, earn, invest, and share.
I am a Soldier of Finance.

We recited the Soldier's Creed as part of the initial ceremony, and then we stepped into training to begin living it. That made it official. We didn't yet possess the skills needed to be *good* soldiers— that would take a little time—but we nevertheless were soldiers. Likewise, you are now officially a Soldier of Finance. Time to train.

FINDING A BATTLE BUDDY

There is a logic to Basic Training that isn't always obvious until you look back. When a drill sergeant was screaming obscenities in my face and ordering me to do push-ups, I got the distinct feeling that he wanted nothing more than to break me down and destroy me. It was during those times that I asked myself, "Why am I here?"

Looking back, I realize that before they ever started yelling, they provided everything we would need to survive the training and come out strong and prepared. The Soldier's Creed answered the question, "Why?" We were there to serve our nation.

An intellectual understanding, however, is not much motivation when you're under pressure. I can guarantee you, I never once thought about the president while the drill sergeant yelled. My drive to perform to the best of my ability came from a desire not to let the buddies in my unit down. If I screwed up, it reflected on them, and I did everything I could to keep that from happening.

Throughout history, memoirs from soldiers everywhere indicate that they never fought for the abstract notion of the motherland. Soldiers fight for each other. Combat forges an immediate and tangible bond between them. They are family. They learn to trust each other, depend on each other, and watch each other's back.

I believe the most important thing the drill instructors did in Basic was push us into supporting each other. One of the first things they did was introduce us to our Battle Buddies. Everyone was assigned another person with whom to form an intimate friendship. We stood in line in alphabetical order, and our Battle Buddy was the person next to us.

That was the guy you got to know. We were required to learn everything about that person. We had to find out if he had brothers or sisters, where he came from, what he did in his childhood, where he went to school, his likes and dislikes.

To impress how important Battle Buddies were, we were subjected to spontaneous quizzes. At any moment, day or night, a drill sergeant could walk up and throw a question at you. "Private Rose, what is your Battle Buddy's father's name?" You had to know the answer. If you didn't, you did push-ups or you got smoked. They knew that mutual support would be absolutely vital when we got into combat. Your Battle Buddy was the person you knew you could absolutely lean on and confide in when you needed it most.

When I went to Iraq, my unit was filled with Battle Buddies. These were the guys I knew would have my back if something happened. If I were injured, they would come and get me. If they were injured, I would come for them. If I needed help, they would be there. If they needed help, I would be there for them. And I knew that if I needed a good butt-kicking, they would do it.

As you step into the shoes of a Soldier of Finance, you will need a Battle Buddy. Let's be brutally honest from the start: The mission you are preparing for will not be easy. Your financial situation is the result of a lifetime of thinking and acting a certain way. Change doesn't just happen. It takes time and effort. You will be faced with obstacles and challenges that you have never wanted to put yourself through.

And you can't do it on your own, no matter how tough you think you are. If you could, you wouldn't be reading this book right now. You will need a support system to back you up.

A Battle Buddy isn't necessarily your best friend. He might be, but more important, he must be someone who will always be honest with you, even if it's unpleasant.

In the military, my Battle Buddies were the guys in my squad. As a Soldier of Finance, my number one Battle Buddy is my wife. She has been the one person I have always been able to confide in, who knows me better than anyone. She understands my goals and what I want to accomplish. She is there to encourage me, to pick me up on days when I'm frustrated or upset, and she's there to cheer me on.

My wife knows my weaknesses and what I need to work on. I've always been more of a spender than a saver. "Frugal" was not a word in my vocabulary through most of my life. My wife, as a good Battle Buddy, keeps me in check.

Of course, being a good Battle Buddy means commitment on my part, too. I know her goals and dreams and I'm there to support them. Naturally, we share goals and we work together to achieve them. When I went overseas, we set a goal of paying off some debt we had acquired, specifically laser eye surgery and her engagement ring. We also committed to building up our savings to $5,000. By communicating those goals and working together, we pushed and encouraged each other, ultimately achieving what we set out to do. I recall that many of our phone conversations during my time in Iraq involved discussing the progress toward our goals, and our excitement when we saw the progress we made. I doubt either one of us could have achieved anywhere near as much on our own. I know I couldn't.

Your Battle Buddy can be a friend, spouse, close family member, or even your financial advisor. The most important thing is honesty. The concept of a Battle Buddy will occur frequently throughout this book. Your Battle Buddy is your cheerleader, your accountability partner, and your conscience.

Before you get too far into the Soldier of Finance training, make sure your support system is in place. If you know anyone who may make a good Battle Buddy, now is a good time to broach the topic with him or her. It's not weakness to acknowledge that you need help. Find a Battle Buddy today and take charge of your life.

IDENTIFYING BLUE FALCONS

Not everyone makes a good Battle Buddy. Because so much trust is involved, you have to be sure the person you choose is trustworthy. And you have to be trustworthy yourself.

We had a term in the military for a soldier who was not a good Battle Buddy. He was a "Blue Falcon."

That rather odd name is an attempt to clean up a much more graphic term. The initials for Blue Falcon, "BF," were originally the first letters of a term I'll refrain from printing here. Let's just say that the "B" stood for "Buddy" and the "F" stood for a classic word of profanity. A BF was someone who screwed his buddies. We just called them Blue Falcons.

To illustrate how this looked in Basic Training, the drill sergeants played a lot of mental games with us. For example, we were often required to stand in formation for as long as thirty or forty minutes at a time. Typically we would be at parade rest or at full attention, with our hands at our sides, heels together, and eyes straight ahead.

Thirty minutes might not seem like a long time, but when you can't even flinch, you start to notice nagging little itches and muscle pains. With drill sergeants lurking behind, an itch can become a torment. Anyone who got caught in the slightest movement brought down the wrath of the drill sergeant immediately, but not just on the person who moved. The entire platoon paid the price, usually by assuming what we euphemistically called the "front-leaning rest position." That meant push-ups, and lots of them.

We could get smoked for a wide variety of infractions. If someone showed up in formation without the proper gear, everyone paid. If someone didn't have his *Soldier's Handbook* in his cargo pocket, everyone paid. If someone didn't have enough water in his canteen, everyone paid. Blue Falcons were those soldiers who got in trouble and everyone paid the price.

It is important that you be aware of Blue Falcons in your life. Choose a Blue Falcon as a Battle Buddy, and you are liable to get screwed.

Understand that the Blue Falcons you are most likely to encounter are not people who want bad things to happen to you. They don't usually think they are doing anything wrong. Often they are your family members, and that often makes it very hard to deal with them.

I loved my dad, but he was a Blue Falcon at times. He not only had bad financial habits himself, but he recommended things to me that would have caused similar problems if I listened to him. Observing how he used his credit cards, for example, I saw that he was constantly in debt and struggling to keep up with the payments. But that didn't mean he recognized his problem. He filed for bankruptcy twice. One time he borrowed $8,000 from me to help pay off some of his debt, and when he realized he wouldn't be able to pay me back, he took out a life insurance policy for that amount with me as the beneficiary.

As my dad got older, the constant stress of struggling with money started to wear on him. I can remember visiting his house and seeing that next to his computer in his home office was a list of all his credit card debt. Each one of them was in the 20% to 30% APR range. He constantly worried about how to make the minimum payments. Often he used one card to make a payment on another. He took cash advances to pay credit card bills. It was a vicious cycle and he never seemed to understand the problem.

In spite of his own financial stress, his was the strongest voice encouraging me to open my first credit card. Throughout my teen years, that was what I believed I needed to do. Soon I had the same kind of debt he struggled with. He genuinely believed it was a good thing for me, but his advice was not in my best interest.

In time, as I began to recognize how poor his spending habits were, I changed my own. However, that didn't automatically eliminate him as a Blue Falcon in my life. When I was 24 years old, my grandmother passed away and my father and I both inherited some money. My dad wanted to borrow my share of the inheritance in order to pay off his debt and get out from under the load he was carrying. He planned to pay it back in monthly installments.

My girlfriend, who later became my wife, proved the value of a good Battle Buddy. She reminded me that he already owed me money from previous loans, and he wasn't paying that back very consistently. "You can't do this," she confronted me. "It won't help him and it won't help you."

That was the first time I ever said no to my dad. I remember the day clearly. It was the hardest thing I had ever done. I sat in the car, cell phone in hand, ready to go to the center where I worked out. I told him no, hung up, and started crying. The emotions of that moment were intense, draining, and disturbing. It was more than the difficulty of saying what needed to be said to a close relative; it was the recognition that he should never have put me in that position in the first place. Blue Falcons set you up for failure if you let them.

You are probably surrounded by Blue Falcons. Most of them mean well, but they don't share your goals. They are the people who influence your behaviors and habits away from where you need to go.

Let's say you make a commitment to budget in order to save some money and take care of a specific debt. This means controlling your spending by watching how many times you eat out each week, what you do for recreational activities on the weekend, and how much you spend on things you don't necessarily need, like new designer clothes.

Blue Falcons in your life are people who pull you away from that commitment. They might be coworkers, or they could be friends or family. As soon as you decide to stop eating out, a Blue Falcon will suggest having dinner at your favorite Mexican restaurant, the one you go to every Thursday night. As soon as you decide to cut back on buying new clothes, a Blue Falcon will invite you to go to the mall, the one with your favorite stores. Blue Falcons will provide you with constant temptations to break your commitment. Battle Buddies will do whatever they can to encourage you to keep your commitment.

Understand that people only qualify as Blue Falcons if you have communicated to them what you are trying to accomplish. If they don't know you are trying to get out of debt, they won't be aware that anything has changed, and they won't do anything different. Being a Soldier of Finance requires that you communicate with people. If they know your goals and still try to influence you to do other things, they are Blue Falcons. If your friends know you have bad spending habits, and they still tell you to charge just one more pair of shoes, they are not Battle Buddies. They are Blue Falcons.

Choosing Battle Buddies requires that you identify the Blue Falcons in your life. Once you know who they are, you will need to either cut ties or at least reduce the amount of time you spend with them and minimize their influence on you. I cannot stress enough how important this is. Be honest with yourself. If you are easily influenced, you will have to admit it to yourself enough to step back and make some changes.

DOWN TO BASICS

We've already covered several extremely important points and we haven't even started the training yet. We've defined why you're here and taken steps to build a reliable support system around you. This will pay important dividends down the road. Success starts with having the right attitude. You are in this to succeed, so lay the right foundation for success. Give yourself the best possible chance of winning. It does matter. It matters to your family, your true friends, and your future. As Vince Lombardi said, "*If it doesn't matter who wins or loses, then why do they keep score?*"

Go / No Go

Soldier of Finance Enlistment Checklist

Are you serious about gaining control of your financial life?

_____ Go _____ No Go

Have you taken the Soldier of Finance Oath?

_____ Go _____ No Go

Have you read the Soldier of Finance Creed?

_____ Go _____ No Go

Have you identified possible Battle Buddies?

_____ Go _____ No Go

Have you talked to the person or people on your list about being your Battle Buddy?

_____ Go _____ No Go

Have you identified Blue Falcons in your life?

_____ Go _____ No Go

SUMMARY

- The Soldier of Finance Oath is an act of commitment to make a change.

- The Soldier of Finance Creed is a statement of personal values and of your mission in life.

- You need a Battle Buddy, someone who will give you encouragement to achieve your goals and also give you honest advice, even when it's unpleasant.

- Blue Falcons are those friends or family members who distract you away from your goals. You need to be aware of who they are.

PART TWO

INITIAL TRAINING PHASE (WEEKS 1–5)

Phase One is designed to gain control of your financial life. The Initial Training Phase involves analyzing your situation and abolishing negative influences. You will identify your weaknesses, bad habits, and debts, and change or eliminate them. By the end of this section, you will be prepared to get yourself out of the red and into a positive cash flow.

WEEK 1

THE ARMY PHYSICAL— MEASURE YOUR DEBT

They specifically tell you to wear underwear . . . And to bathe, or shower, the night before. That may seem trivial, but I suppose when they get to the part of the exam where they tell you to strip down to your boxers, they don't want any surprises. Before they're done, even the underwear won't keep anything hidden.

That is my primary memory of MEPS, the Military Entrance Processing Station. Before they administer the oath, the Army wants to know everything about you. Try to hide anything and you'll either end up heading home or sitting in jail. They take it pretty seriously. Skeletons in the closet won't necessarily keep you out of the Army, but trying to keep them secret definitely will. The recruiter will have already asked a truckload of questions; if there was anything you didn't want them to find out, something you had done in your past, they would find out anyway.

That worried me. I had always thought I had flat feet or kind of low arches. People had warned me it could be a problem. To cover it, they recommended that I stand with the pressure on the outside of my feet, creating the illusion of natural arches. I tried it, but honestly, I don't think it made much difference. If it were really a problem, they would have seen it.

First came the Medical Questionnaire, with questions about everything that had ever happened to me, every broken bone, every serious cut, every disease—everything. That was before the physical.

We were given blood and urine tests, hearing tests, and eye exams. We were weighed to ensure that we were within the accepted standards. If we had anything in our blood system, from alcohol to HIV, they found it.

About thirty of us were herded into a room and told to strip down to our boxers. At that point they would know if we had neglected to put on underwear, and they would probably know whether or not we showered.

They inspected us for scars or skin abnormalities, deformities, pelvic tilt, scoliosis, leg length discrepancies, and flat feet. Apparently I didn't have any.

We were guided through a whole range of odd exercises— making full arm circles, flexing our elbows, touching our thumbs to our shoulders, and bending over to touch our toes. They watched carefully, ascertaining whether we had a normal range of motion and flexibility. Any signs of pain or discomfort from the movements and they would know something was wrong. Having us raise one leg in the air or stand on our toes and walk around tested our balance.

Once satisfied that we weren't crippled in any way, they moved us on to the next part of the physical. A doctor interviewed each one of us, complete with poking and probing into every cavity he could find.

I hated it at the time, but I recognized that the Army needed to know if there were any potential problems. They were about to invest a lot of money and time into training me, and did not want to get six weeks in and find out I had a back problem that would keep me hospitalized for the duration of my enlistment.

YOUR FINANCIAL STATUS: STOP BEING IN DENIAL

As a Soldier of Finance, you must complete a thorough examination of your current financial status. You can't plan your future without understanding your present. If you have financial skeletons in your closet, you need to acknowledge them now. You have to swallow hard and admit that you made some poor financial decisions. If you have a lot of student loan debt or high credit card balances and no savings, it's time to stop being in denial.

Don't run from your financial skeletons; embrace them before they ruin your future. Instead of living in dread of them, use them as inspiration to push you to where you need to be.

DEBRIEFING

The Meaning of *"Not Much Debt"*

I am consistently amazed how often people don't know how much debt they have. Not long ago, I met with a couple planning for retirement. They were about five to ten years out with plenty of time to prepare and I was impressed that they were thinking ahead. Many people wait until it's too late to do much for them. I happily sat down to help them plan their financial goals.

I met with the wife, since her husband was working that day, and started with a few basic questions, to get an idea of what we had to work with. It was all fairly routine.

"How much debt do you have?" I asked.

"Oh, we don't have a lot of debt," she responded.

"How much do you have?" I continued, trying to get a specific amount nailed down.

"Oh, I don't know exactly, our house is paid off and we don't have much else."

I began to get excited. As a financial planner, when someone tells me that their mortgage is paid off and they have minimal consumer debt, I start thinking the possibilities are really good. We looked at their savings, and while I would have preferred a little more, it looked like they were in good shape. I thought, *"This is impressive."*

I needed more precise figures, however, to really plan, so I sent her home with an assignment to gather all the information on any debt they still had. Then the truth came out. I opened her e-mail and was floored by what she thought was *"not much debt."*

First she listed their car loans. Not one, but two, totaling about $15,000. Then she said they also had a camper on which they still owed $10,000. To top it off, they had credit card debt totaling $25,000. Altogether, that amounted to $50,000 of consumer debt, hardly a small amount! To make it worse, some of the credit cards were from department stores where they paid interest from 18% up into the 20% range.

Suddenly the conversation went from *"not much debt"* to *"a lot of debt."* To make matters worse, the husband didn't know how much debt they had, given his wife took care of the bills. He was working at his job, dreaming of retirement in a few years with plenty of savings and no financial worries. Suddenly that was in jeopardy.

This couple illustrates the problem, but they are hardly alone. An amazing number of people are in the same position. I frequently hear young people in college talk about their student loans. "Oh, I only have $15,000 in debt."

"Only" $15,000? That's a lot of debt! And for most students it's even higher. They often have credit card debt and a car loan on top of that.

If you have any consumer debt at all, it's too much. Take the steps to eliminate as much of it as you can, as fast as you can.

THE SITUATION REPORT

The Army physical was not pleasant. No one likes having everything about them exposed, even to themselves. But it is absolutely vital to success. You can't fix something if you don't know it needs fixing.

If the Army finds something wrong, you're sent home, and that's it. Fortunately, as a Soldier of Finance, you get the opportunity to correct the problem before it creates greater hardship. Living in denial won't get you anywhere. If there are skeletons in your financial closet, you need to know they're there. Debt is an enemy to your future, and you need a plan to combat it.

The most important ingredient of a tactical or strategic decision is information. A general cannot coordinate the movements of an army without knowing where the enemy is, how strong he is, and the direction in which he is moving. What that means is that one of the most important things a soldier can do is report information. When I was on duty in Iraq, most of our patrols were for the purpose of keeping track of what was happening around us, so that information was as accurate and current as possible. We were trained from the beginning to observe and report.

The basic form we used was called a Spot Report, or SPOTREP for short. A SPOTREP was a report we were expected to submit within five minutes of observing enemy activity. We were trained to use the SALUTE format to make sure we didn't miss anything important. SALUTE is an acronym for:

S = **Size.** Report the number of personnel, vehicles, aircraft, or the size of an object.

A = **Activity.** Report a detailed account of actions such as direction of movement, troops digging in, artillery fire, and type of attack.

L = **Location.** Report where you saw the activity.

U = **Unit or Uniform.** Report the identity of the enemy unit, if you can tell. If not, report any distinctive features such as uniforms, patches, headgear, and vehicle markings.

T = **Time.** Report the time of your observation.

E = **Equipment.** Report all equipment associated with the activity, such as weapons, vehicles, and tools.

With the Spot Report in hand, officers could make informed decisions about how to handle enemy movements. Since debt is the enemy of the Soldier of Finance, our goal is to gain a clear understanding of what we face.

A Soldier of Finance needs accurate information. At this point, we are going to create a variation of the Spot Report, which we'll call the Debt Situation Report. We'll shorten that to the SIT Report, to make it easy to remember. That stands for:

S = Size of the debt

I = Interest rate

T = Type of debt

In order to complete this report, list every debt you have. Begin with the size of the debt and include the amount you owe on it and the interest rate you're paying. You might be shocked when you see how much you're paying every month beyond the principal. Include the amount of your monthly payment, to make sure you know how much is going out every month. (If you want to insert "Payment" into the acronym, that would make it a SPIT Report, which could be more appropriate.) Finally, list the type of debt—credit card, car loan, student loan, etc.

Your SIT Report should include every debt you write a check for each month. If you're making a payment, it's a debt. Your goal here is to answer questions you've avoided for too long:

- How much debt do you really have?

- How many credit cards do you have?

- What are the interest rates on those cards?

- Do you have a student loan, and what is the interest rate on it?

- How much is your mortgage, and what interest rate are you paying?

Jotting down all of your debts and all of your interest rates will give a clear snapshot of your current position. Step one in training is to look at the real picture. Don't worry about how to fix things. We'll get to that soon enough. First, uncover the truth. Just as the Army physical reveals every flaw, you need to be brutally honest and transparent as you examine your financial situation. You don't have to physically stand naked in front of a doctor, but you do have to take a hard look at your reality—no matter how embarrassing it might be.

WARRIOR TASK
Complete Your SIT Report

Complete the following SIT Report. List all your debts and relevant details.

Size of the Debt   Interest (%)   Type of Debt (credit card, car loan, etc.)

1. _____   _____   _____

2. _____ _____ _____

3. _____ _____ _____

4. _____ _____ _____

5. _____ _____ _____

6. _____ _____ _____

P/X RANGERS (OR LIVING BEYOND YOUR MEANS)

In October 2008, Steve Burton, an information technology specialist at a bank in Palm Springs, attended his twentieth high school class reunion. He walked in the door like a conquering hero, decked out in a Marine dress uniform with lieutenant colonel insignia and a mass of medals, including a Purple Heart, a Bronze Star, the Legion of Merit, and the Navy Cross, the highest medal awarded exclusively by the Navy.

A year later, he was in U.S. District Court, charged with impersonating a U.S. Marine and with wearing unauthorized medals.

As it turned out, Burton has never served in any branch of the military. The medals had been purchased on eBay and at military surplus stores. He had a picture taken of himself in the uniform on the beach at Coronado Island. He blogged extensively about service in Afghanistan and Iraq, although he had never been there.

Everyone was deeply impressed at the reunion, and Burton was the center of attention; a little more attention than he bargained for, as it turned out. A woman who actually was a Navy commander knew how rarely the Navy Cross is awarded. It is only given for *"extreme gallantry and risk of life, beyond the call of duty, performed in combat with an enemy force."* She was a little suspicious, so she asked Burton if he would pose for a picture with her.

He agreed and she took the picture to the FBI. They investigated and brought charges. In early 2010, Burton was fined $250 and sentenced to a one-year probation.

The crime is considered a misdemeanor, carrying a maximum of one year in jail. That might seem a little harsh for someone playing dress-up, but those who have served in combat wouldn't agree. They take their service seriously and don't appreciate anyone claiming accomplishments when they never were in actual danger of being shot at. Phonies are not well liked. We had a name for them: *PX Rangers.*

PX stands for "Post Exchange." It is the general store on an Army base, where you can buy virtually anything you need. Included in the inventory are all the ribbons, badges, and decorations worn on uniforms. If you need something for your uniform, you go to the PX and buy it.

If you were a Ranger, for example, you would wear a Ranger tab on your left arm. The Rangers are the elite of the elite. They

go through hardcore training that most people could never endure. If you saw a Ranger, you knew he was a stud. Very few could qualify to wear that Ranger tab.

Yet anyone could buy the tab. You just walked into the PX, picked it up, and paid for it. We used to joke that someone might not be tough enough to be a Ranger, but he could easily become a PX Ranger. You could buy the badge, put it on your sleeve, and no one would suspect—except an actual Ranger. If a real Ranger found out, you would not be able to run fast enough to get away. It would not be a good thing.

The question you must answer in this chapter is: *Am I a financial PX Ranger?* How can you tell? You've heard the phrase "keeping up with the Joneses," meaning you try to live beyond your means in order to have the appearance of success. If your neighbor has a new car, you feel compelled to get a new car, just to look good. Your brother-in-law buys a big-screen TV, so you have to get a big-screen TV, just so he won't think you're a failure when he comes by your house. The reality, however, is that you are over-leveraged and maxed out. Your appearance of success is a fraud.

Examining your financial situation does not serve to beat you up for poor financial management. The objective is to get to the truth. If your SIT Report shows that you have an exorbitant amount of consumer debt, then you know exactly what enemy you need to attack to bring your finances under control.

Do not buy into the illusion of success. Instead, aim for the substance of real success. Step on the financial scale and take a long, hard look at your weaknesses. Be honest in creating your own Situation Report; when you do, you will be able to recognize your reality. Put away those shiny medals and ribbons and get ready to develop a winning strategy that will put you back in charge of your life.

You can access the SIT Report form on the Soldier of Finance website at www.soldieroffinance.com/resources.

Go / No Go

Performance Measure

Have you completed your SIT Report?

_____ **Go**   _____ **No Go**

Have you analyzed the amount of credit card debt you have?

_____ **Go**   _____ **No Go**

Do you have debt for things you don't need? Do you have debt because you want to appear wealthy?

_____ **Go**   _____ **No Go**

SUMMARY

- As a Soldier of Finance, you need to complete a thorough examination of your current financial status.

- Don't be in denial about your true financial status.

- A Debt Situation Report (SIT Report) will help you analyze your current debt situation. SIT stands for Size of the debt, Interest rate, and Type of debt.

- Do not be a financial PX Ranger, trying to pretend you are wealthier than you are. Keeping up with the Joneses for the sake of appearance will produce unnecessary and often crippling debt.

WEEK 2

ROSTER NUMBER—YOUR CREDIT SCORE FOR LIFE

"Private, what's your roster number?"

That was never a question I wanted to hear. It meant I was in trouble.

"First Sergeant! Roster number four-zero-three," I barked out. *"Oh, crap,"* I thought. *"I'm screwed."*

Most of the time I managed to fly under the radar. The last thing you want during training is to be noticed. And at that moment, I had definitely been noticed. "Four zero three" was my numerical identification, which was more important than my name. "Four" indicated I belonged to the fourth platoon, and "zero three" meant I was the third person when the fourth platoon lined up. At that moment, I was the only one being noticed.

We were in a typical formation, standing at attention, heels to-gether, arms to our sides with thumbs resting on the seams of our pants, eyes straight ahead. As often happened, the drill sergeant walked away for thirty minutes or more and left us standing. It was a test, of course. We could not talk, scratch, or sneeze. Absolutely no movement was allowed.

My first sergeant had seen me talking. "Four zero three? I'll re-member that number," he said. "We'll be talking soon." My only hope was that he would forget, but "403" isn't hard to remember . . . which he did. The next day we were out at a range and I heard the first sergeant's voice: "Where's 403? We need to talk."

Needless to say, he did all the talking. I did push-ups while nine other drill sergeants watched. From that moment on, I dreaded hear-ing my number. I got smoked systematically until some other private screwed up and became the next victim. By that time, I was almost smoked out.

Roster numbers were assigned at Basic Training and they followed us everywhere. I was either "Private Rose" or "Number 403." My number predetermined where I lined up in just about anything, from where I stood in the chow line to where I drew weapons to where I stood or marched in a formation. My number was everywhere. I wrote it on my *Soldier's Handbook.* It was plastered on every piece of gear, on my Kevlar, helmet, weapon, canteen—*everywhere!* As my pri-mary identifier, my roster number was more important than my name.

As a Soldier of Finance, you also have an identifying number that is, in many ways, more important than your name: your credit score. It is tied to everything financial and follows you everywhere you go. It is plastered on every loan application and every apartment rental. The good thing about credit scores is that, unlike Army roster num-bers, they don't stay the same (I earnestly wanted to change my roster number a couple of times). Our credit scores are not locked in. They can be changed if we take action to improve them.

740 IS THE NEW 720

For all practical purposes, your credit score is your financial identity. Note that there is a difference between a credit "score" and a credit "report." Your credit report, which we will discuss in Chapter 5, is a snapshot of your credit use history. Your credit score is a three-digit number based on the information from your credit report. You will often see it called a FICO score, from the name of the company that computes it, Fair Isaac Corporation.

After the credit bureaus take into account all aspects of your report, a mathematical formula is used to determine your score. No one really knows quite how a credit score is computed except the people at Fair Isaac. What you do need to know is the primary factors that are included in the calculation. These include:

- Payment history

- Balances on loans and credit cards

- Length of your credit history

- New credit

- Types of credit used

Lenders refer to this little number to determine your creditworthiness. It will affect whether or not you will be approved for a mortgage or car loan. And if you do get the loan, your credit score will affect how much interest you pay. Moreover, any loan you apply for triggers a credit check, the results of which will affect the interest rate you get and whether or not you're approved for the loan in the first place.

Your credit information will affect things you likely haven't thought about. For example, it will dictate the kinds of credit cards you can obtain and how much interest you pay on them. Landlords, in deciding who gets an apartment and who does not, utilize credit scores. Insurance companies use them to evaluate applicants and set their premiums. Even prospective employers check your credit score to help them determine whether you might steal from them once you start working. Your credit score plays an important role in nearly every aspect of your life. It represents all the past financial decisions you have made, which is also a reflection on your character.

The higher your credit score number, the better your credit. A score of 720 used to be the number that would garner the best loan terms, and even if the score was lower, decent deals could still be found. Since the economy tanked, credit has tightened considerably. To guarantee the best deals, you now need at least a 740. And if your credit score is bad, you're out of luck.

CREDIT SCORES AND YOUR MORTGAGE

To give you an idea why these three digits are so important, let's look at something as basic as a mortgage payment. Table 4-1 shows the differences in monthly payments on a thirty-year fixed mortgage for different FICO scores on a $300,000 mortgage.

The difference between the top bracket, with scores between 760 and 850, and the bottom, with scores under 640, is more than 1.5 percent. That might not seem like much until you realize that the difference in monthly payments is $276. That means that over the full thirty years of the mortgage, the person with the low credit score will pay a grand total of almost $100,000 more for the exact same home. Of course, that assumes he can get the mortgage in the first place.

The good news is that over the thirty years, the homeowner will probably improve his credit score and likely refinance, thus reducing both his interest rate and monthly payment. So if your credit score is low, all is not lost. But the higher you can get your FICO number, the better off you will be.

Table 4-1 ■ Effect of Credit Score on Mortgage Payment

FICO Score	APR	Monthly Mortgage Payment
760–850	3.288%	$1,312
700–759	3.510%	$1,349
680–699	3.687%	$1,379
660–679	3.901%	$1,415
640–659	4.331%	$1,490
620–639	4.877%	$1,588

FINDING YOUR CREDIT SCORE

Getting your credit score is not difficult, but there will be a small cost. The easiest time to find your score is when you get your credit report, which you will learn to do in Chapter 5. I will cover the details of getting your credit score at that point.

For now, be aware that there are several kinds of credit scores available, including your consumer score, a rental score, and an auto formula score. Make sure you get the right number. You want your FICO score. That is the number used by nine out of ten lenders, and it is generally lower than some of the other numbers. If you get a consumer score, thinking it is your FICO score, you will likely be off by as much as a couple of hundred points.

There are three credit reporting bureaus that provide credit reports free of charge and credit scores for a small fee. They are TransUnion, Experian, and Equifax. If you buy a credit score from Experian, it will be a consumer credit score. TransUnion and Equifax will provide you with the FICO score.

You can refer to www.soldieroffinance.com/resources to find trusted sites from which to request your credit score. There are plenty of other sites that will give you a credit score, but they aren't your real FICO score. The only advantage is that they give you a rough idea of how your credit is, but they aren't what lenders will pull.

Go / No Go

Credit Score Definition

Do you know your credit score?

_____ **Go**   _____ **No Go**

Do you understand that a FICO score is different from your consumer credit score?

_____ **Go**   _____ **No Go**

SUMMARY

- Your credit score, a three-digit number based on information in your credit report, is your financial identity.

- Your credit score reflects your payment history, balances on loans and credit cards, length of your credit history, new credit, and types of credit you have used.

- A credit score of at least 740 is required to secure the best deals.

- You can get your credit score when you obtain your credit report, but there will be a charge.

- Be sure you get your FICO score, not a consumer, rental, or auto score.

WEEK 3

LAND MINES—
YOUR CREDIT REPORT

As trained infantry soldiers, we knew that our feet were our main mode of transportation. Everywhere we went, we were on our boots. In modern combat, soldiers move around in vehicles like Humvees, but our training prepared us for walking. In real-life military scenarios, one of the dangers of being on foot is stepping into a minefield, so naturally we trained for that situation. It was one of the most annoying exercises we had to learn.

When you're confronted with a minefield, there are three options. The first is to cry, which was not really an option given to us soldiers. Anyone who actually cried would be thrown into the minefield by the drill instructor.

The second option, if you're already in the minefield before realizing it, is to retrace your footsteps, turning around and walking back exactly the way you came. The object is to step only where you have already stepped, so you look for your footprint and step into it. This option is only good if you can afford to go back the way you came. If your mission is to support some other operation, you don't have a choice. You have to move forward.

Of course, the best way to avoid problems with a mine is simply to not step on it. The trouble with that option is that mines are hidden under the surface of the ground, and they're not easily located. Fortunately, if you know how to look for them, they can be found.

To begin the search, you use your hands to smooth out the grass in front of you. Hopefully, if there is a mine under the surface, you can feel enough of a bump to recognize it. Then you either get down on your knees or lie in a prone position.

Once you know the immediate area is safe, you begin probing. During training, that meant using our bayonets—long Rambo knives attached to the ends of our M-16s—inserting the blade into the

ground at an angle (probing straight down could set off a mine). Covering one area at a time, we pushed the blade in deep enough to detect any hard objects beneath the surface.

Eventually the "ding" of my blade hitting something would cause my breath to catch as I hoped that what I hit was just a rock. If we did find a mine, we marked it so that EOD (Explosive Ordnance Disposal) could remove it safely and securely.

As tense and exciting as it was when the bayonet clinked against something, probing a minefield was mostly tedious and exhausting. It took forever to cover a small amount of ground. I can remember spending almost an entire day, with the drill sergeants standing over us. At the end of the exercise, I was worn out.

Annoying and miserable as those days were, I would rather suffer through them than step on a mine. World War II tales depict peasants on the Eastern Front being herded across minefields ahead of the regular troops. Most lost their lives in the process. The fastest way to discover a mine is to start walking, but the price isn't worth it. Given the choice, I'd rather start probing, no matter how long it takes or how annoying it is.

The point of this illustration is that what you can't see and what you don't know about *can* hurt you. And when it comes to your credit report, you might be surprised to find what is there.

MY FIRST CREDIT REPORT

The first time I probed into my credit report, I didn't really expect to find anything. I was young and hadn't done much yet. But I was curious, so I requested a copy. Right away I found an error. The report said I was delinquent on payments for a gym membership. I had canceled the membership five years earlier and didn't even live in the same state anymore! When I was a member, I never missed a payment, but somehow, the records got mixed up. And there it was on my credit report, pulling down my credit score.

It wasn't difficult to fix. I made a phone call and sent a letter and it was done. The point is, if I had never probed my credit report for land mines, that one would have blown up in my face somewhere down the road. It would have continued to hurt my credit rating going forward.

According to a Consumer Action study, 27 percent of Americans have never checked their credit reports. Now for the sobering part: Among the credit reports surveyed by the U.S. Public Interest Research Group (PIRG), 25 percent contained serious errors that could result in the denial of credit. Altogether, 79 percent of credit reports surveyed contained an error or mistake of some kind. And those errors affect your credit score.

It is very important that you check your credit report at least once a year. The only way you can be sure the information on it is accurate is to check it. Who knows what land mines are lurking there? It takes time, but you need to probe into it so there are no surprises down the road. This needs to become a regular part of your financial reconnaissance.

According to FINRA (Financial Industry Regulatory Authority), only 42 percent of people have obtained a copy of their credit report. Even fewer have checked their credit score in the past twelve months. These statistics are unacceptable, considering how easy it is to check. I suspect that most people are afraid of what they'll find, but now that you've gone through your financial physical and filled out your SIT Report, doing this should be easy.

WHERE TO GET YOUR FREE CREDIT REPORT

Several corporations are in the business of reporting credit, but three in particular are the primary sources for most people: TransUnion, Experian, and Equifax. Fortunately, the law requires that those three major credit reporting agencies allow you to check your credit once a year at no cost. You can check all three at once or you can spread it out by checking one every four months. Regardless of which method you choose, you absolutely must do it.

The big three credit reporting agencies jointly sponsor a website, www.AnnualCreditReport.com, where every twelve months you can request a copy of each of your credit reports. If you want to keep track of how often you have requested reports, set up calendar reminders on Google Calendar, MS Outlook, or some other calendar system.

The procedure is simple. You will be asked some basic information to verify your identity, including your name, address, and Social Security number. After completing your personal information, you will be asked to select the credit bureau from which you want to receive a report.

Once you make that selection, you will be transferred to the website for the company you chose. After you fill out the necessary personal information, your credit report will show up on the screen with an option to print. If you opt to print your report, be sure to select the option to show only the last four digits of your Social Security number on the personal information page. That way you won't have your full number on a paper that potentially can be lost or stolen.

You can also request that your credit report be mailed to you, if you prefer, or if you don't have access to a printer. It takes about fifteen days for the request to be processed and sent to you. If you're not comfortable giving your information online, you can call them toll free at 1-877-322-8228.

Obtaining your credit score is more difficult than getting a credit report, but it can be done. Of course, if you don't mind paying a few dollars, you can request it at the same time you print your report. The credit reporting companies don't mind charging you for things that are legally allowed. This is where you should be on your guard, because the companies plant a few land mines of their own. Often they offer an option to sign up for a free trial period for their other services in return for a free credit score. You then have a period of time, usually a week or thirty days, to cancel before you are charged.

If you order your credit score, be sure that you obtain the correct number. You want the FICO score, since that is the number used by at least 90 percent of lenders. But as you learned in Chapter 4, there are three other types of credit scores available—the consumer score, the rental score, and the auto formula score. If you are looking at your consumer credit score, thinking it is your FICO score, you could easily think your score is a couple of hundred points higher than what a lender sees. The Experian score is a consumer credit score; you can get the FICO score from TransUnion and Equifax. Many people get a credit score from the website www.AnnualCreditReport.com, but that is a consumer score, *not* FICO.

CAREFULLY VERIFY THE INFORMATION

Be prepared for a shock. Your credit report is a long document. The first time I printed mine, it was over thirty pages. I didn't think I had lived long enough for that much information to accumulate. Every detail of my financial history, from the first day I got credit, was preserved there. I felt overwhelmed.

Then I remembered my enlistment physical. The United States Army not only wanted to know everything about me, they kept it in a file so that no detail would ever get lost. Every shot they gave me was recorded. Every injury, infection, medical procedure, and exam was written down. Every award I received is in that file. Every score on every test I took is there. Everything that happened to me from Basic Training through my tour in Iraq is preserved forever. That file is *me!*

Your credit report is the same. For all financial purposes, that report is you. Your credit *score* is your roster number and your credit *report* is your financial identity. In your credit report, you can expect to find:

- Your personal information (name, address, Social Security number, etc.)

- Types of credit you use or have used (credit cards, mortgages, loans)

- How long each individual line of credit has been open

- Whether you have paid your bills on time (including any collection information if a debt was passed on to a collection agency)

- How much of the credit you have used, and what is outstanding

- Whether you have been looking to open new sources of credit (any credit inquiries that have been made, such as when you apply for credit)

- Banking information

- Public records (such as bankruptcy or a court-related judgment)

Take the time to go through this information in the same manner in which you would examine a minefield. Go slowly and look at *everything*. Search for errors, and take note of your financial habits. Errors can be corrected and bad habits can be changed, but you have to catch them first.

Be vigilant! Your name might be misspelled, potentially creating identity problems. Addresses are not always current. You could be listed as working for a specific employer when you quit the job long ago. Look for accounts that are not yours, or accounts that you no longer have . . . like a gym membership.

Examine your report for any delinquencies on payments. Perhaps you were late on a credit card or a mortgage payment. Make sure that the reports of late payments are accurate. Sometimes you make the payment on time and it still ends up on your report as delinquent.

Check dates on negative items. If a bankruptcy is more than ten years old, it should not be there. Most other defaults should disappear after seven years. Make sure nothing is on your credit report that shouldn't be there.

One of the most harmful and common things on your credit report is a duplicate entry. This can occur easily. If you are late paying a bill and you let it go until it goes to a collection agency, your delinquency is registered on your account. If you still don't pay it—and many people don't with bills such as credit cards—eventually that agency will sell the debt to another collection agency. When the transfer is made, the debt is recorded again, meaning you will have two entries for the same debt.

A significant red flag is the appearance of erroneous personal information. If you see someone else's Social Security number, for example, that could be indicative of identity fraud, or that your report has accidentally been merged with someone else's.

Another common problem is that credit card companies often report credit card limits incorrectly. I will explain why this is a serious problem when we discuss credit cards, but you should carefully check that all of your limits are reported accurately. If your limit is $10,000 and the credit card company reports it as $5,000, it changes the utilization ratio (you will learn more about this in Chapter 6). A balance that is actually 30 percent of your credit limit will appear as 60 percent, which will cause a drop in your credit score.

SET UP YOUR RECON

Gathering intelligence is the most important part of planning any military operation. Likewise, you cannot improve your credit score if you do not keep up with the information in your credit report.

Now that you know how to check your report, there is no excuse for not keeping your eye on it.

Errors found on your credit report should be disputed as quickly as possible. This is not complicated, but it does require that you contact the credit reporting agency and the creditor. You can start with phone calls to clarify any questions you may have, but you will most likely need to write a letter to the creditor and each agency explaining the item you are disputing. Include copies (not originals) of any documents that support your claim. I recommend sending the letters by certified mail so that you have proof they were received.

Credit reporting companies (sometimes referred to as "bureaus") will investigate your claims, usually within thirty days, unless they consider your claims to be frivolous. If the issue is decided in your favor, you can ask that they send a notice of the change to your credit report to anyone who has requested the report in the past six months.

Never assume that your report is correct. Keep up a regular reconnaissance by checking your report at least once a year. You could save yourself a lot of money.

WARRIOR TASK
Obtain Credit Report

- Log on to the website www.AnnualCreditReport.com.

- Find one of the big three credit reporting companies.

- Follow the instructions for obtaining your free credit report.

- Print out the report and read through it carefully, looking for errors.

Go / No Go

Credit Report Check

Have you obtained your credit report in the past year?

_____ **Go**   _____ **No Go**

Is the personal information on your credit report accurate?

_____ **Go**   _____ **No Go**

Does your credit report show late payments? Are they really payments you made late?

_____ **Go**   _____ **No Go**

Are there negative items in your credit report that should have been removed?

_____ **Go**   _____ **No Go**

Are there duplicate entries on your credit report?

_____ **Go**   _____ **No Go**

SUMMARY

- A credit report is a history of your credit habits.

- As many as three-fourths of credit reports have errors that pull down credit scores.

- You need to regularly check your credit report.

- TransUnion, Experian, and Equifax are the best-known credit reporting companies. They will each provide a free credit report once a year. You also can obtain your credit score from them for a small fee.

- Make sure you get your true FICO score and not an impostor.

- You can request your credit report at www.AnnualCredit Report.com.

- Your report will contain personal information, types of credit you use, how long you have had lines of credit, whether or not you have paid bills on time, credit balances and available credit, banking information, and other public records.

- Make sure that you check your credit report for errors.

WEEK 4

THE LOW CRAWL— CREDIT REPAIR

Part of our Army training consisted of learning the Military Low Crawl. I suppose it would have been pleasant if I liked the taste of dirt, but I didn't. Our drill sergeants, however, loved it! So, naturally, we spent a lot of time crawling.

The Low Crawl meant flattening ourselves face down on the ground, as low as possible, and dragging ourselves forward for long periods of time. The object was to stay as invisible as possible when approaching the enemy. To move, we extended our arms forward and slid our legs as far to the side and forward as we could without raising them from the ground. Then, using only our arms and legs, we slid forward along the ground.

The process is slow and methodical, and (hopefully) not very conspicuous. You don't want your enemy to know you are there. If you got too high or put your head up too far, that's when you could be seen and shot. The thing I most remember about the Low Crawl was that it took a lot of energy and I never felt like I was going anywhere.

This is not much different from how people feel when they first tackle the problem of fixing bad credit. It takes time, and you might not feel like you're getting very far. But steady progress is the only way you can get there. Don't be discouraged. Your credit can be fixed, no matter how bad it is. Not unlike making your way through a minefield, you cannot hurry through your credit repair.

Don't expect major results overnight. If you are able to pay down significant amounts of debt quickly, you might see some quick changes in your score, but most likely, it will take time. How much time depends on what is on your credit report. If there are some serious marks, such as bankruptcies or foreclosures, you might not see a great credit score until enough time has passed for those items to drop off the report. Most things drop off the report after seven years, but bankruptcies are there for ten. A few hits, such as applications for certain jobs or for large amounts of insurance, stay on your record indefinitely.

The Low Crawl is slow, and so is credit repair. In time, you do cover ground. Stick with it and you can regain a good credit score. Don't give up. The sooner you start, the sooner you'll get there.

A word of warning: Now that you're thinking about your credit, I have no doubt you will notice advertisements for quick ways to improve your credit score. *Do not fall for them.* They might improve your score a little in the short term, but down the road, unless you make changes in your credit history, the "fix" will be short-lived.

STOP THE BLEEDING

It doesn't take much to start improving your credit score. You can raise it if you work at it. There are a few essential steps you will need to take, and you must understand how credit works.

First, if you can't pay your bills, you can't establish a good credit record. The initial step is to get your financial life under control. Using the information from your SIT Report, assess your position. (If you haven't already done your SIT Report, see Chapter 3.) If your monthly debt payments are more than you are making, you will have to make some changes, such as getting a part-time job for a while or consolidating debts if you can. Trading in your expensive car for a cheaper one that you can afford could also prove prudent. Whatever it takes, you must be realistic about your position and act accordingly.

You may need to make some lifestyle changes. If you eat out a lot, learn how to cook. Everyone needs recreation time, but if you can't pay for expensive concert tickets or a day at a sporting event and still make your payments, find a less expensive form of relaxation, at least until your situation becomes manageable.

The most important thing to remember is that having credit cards and installment loans on your credit record demonstrates that you can be trusted to repay your debts, but only if you fulfill all the commitments you made when you took the loan. To keep your credit score high, you cannot miss payments. Ever.

MY UNNECESSARY DEBT

I wish I could tell you that I have never gotten into unnecessary debt. But I have, which is how I know you can get it under control. I've done it.

The worst debt I've ever had came from the years I was in college. The National Guard paid my tuition and fees, and I had my one-weekend-a-month military service bringing in some money, in addition to a part-time job. There was absolutely no reason for me to get into debt.

Unfortunately, I inherited my father's money skills. I started applying for credit cards from a few local department stores. The Buckle, a clothing boutique for the young and trendy, was one of my favorites. Since I was young, I felt a great need to be trendy. It didn't take long to max out my card. Other cards weren't as bad, but I carried balances on all of them from month to month.

Then a friend educated me on the ease of getting student loans. My college was completely paid for, so I had absolutely no need for the loan, but I discovered all I had to do was apply and it was mine. It was easier than a payday loan. I filled out a couple of applications and within weeks a check for $2,700 arrived in the mail, with absolutely no requirements. I could spend it on anything I wanted. And I didn't have to begin to pay it back until after I graduated.

Three semesters on, I suddenly had student loans of more than $10,000. By that time my credit cards were up to $8,000. That's a lot of debt with virtually nothing to show for it other than a lot of junk that I not only didn't need, but wasn't worth $18,000.

My dilemma hit me one day and I became angry with myself when I realized how far I had let myself go. Enough was enough. I couldn't blame the credit card companies for extending the credit to me. It was my own fault that I bought things. I couldn't blame the government for giving me a student loan that I had no business applying for in the first place. I vowed I would never do that again. With the help of my future wife, I made a plan to pay it off. I felt lucky to graduate with only $18,000 in debt. I realize many people rely on student loans to finance their education. If you genuinely need it, I understand, but most people build up far more debt than they need to. Most of the things we buy, we do not *need*.

PAY DOWN YOUR DEBT

There is only one way to really improve your credit score: by paying off your debt. If your debt balances are too high, you run a much larger risk of being hit with the inability to keep up, resulting in collection calls and a direct hit on your FICO score. The faster you pay it off, the faster your credit will improve.

No magic formula exists for paying down debt. The first step is to stop incurring more. Next, take a look at your debt and see how you can optimize it. Do you have credit cards that you can use to complete a balance transfer, saving on interest immediately? If you found errors on your credit report, your newly improved credit score may give you the option of refinancing at lower interest rates. Any time you can move credit card debt from the card to an installment loan, you will likely be better off.

Once you have explored these options, focus on paying off one debt at a time. Based on your cash flow, budget, and list of debts, devise a plan to reduce your debt as quickly as possible. This is where your SIT Report will be useful in a positive way.

If you can pay more on a loan than the minimum monthly payment, start paying down the principal. You need to make the required payments on all of your loans, of course, but if your cash flow allows, place extra focus on eliminating one debt. Which one you choose to focus on will depend on the size of the loan and the interest rate you are paying. The higher the interest, the more desirable it is to eliminate the debt.

The longer you practice this discipline, the faster your debts will disappear. And one day you will breathe a sigh of relief that you are no longer getting calls or angry letters from creditors. You have regained control of that part of your life.

DEBRIEFING

No Credit to Good Credit

One of the hardest aspects of building good credit is the fact that high debt lowers your credit score, but so does no debt. I had an intern recently who was ready to graduate from college debt free. He had no credit cards, which was good, but he also had no credit. We were talking one day about his financial prospects, and as a matter of course, I asked him, "What is your credit score?"

"I don't know," he replied.

That's not unusual. Most people don't know, and he had never applied for anything that required checking his score. But since I asked, we decided to run a free check. His score was a very low 621. Since anything under 650 is considered bad credit, we felt that we should take a look at it.

This kid had been completely dependable and responsible about his finances, yet his credit score was horrible. His parents had advised him not to get a credit card, and he followed their advice. Unfortunately, if you don't use credit, you can't establish a credit history. A decent credit score requires that you demonstrate you have handled credit in the past. There must be a record of making payments. A good credit score results from showing that you can incur debt and be responsible for paying it off on time.

(Continues on next page)

His first attempt to secure a credit card was rejected. He approached a couple of banks, and after he told them he was unemployed and had no credit history, they laughed at him.

One of the banks that denied him offered good advice that set him on the right track. First, they told him to stop applying for credit. Every time a credit check had been run, it lowered his credit score. Part of the credit bureau calculation is the number of credit checks run.

He then applied for a secured credit card. There are numerous options for this. In his case, it was a card offered through Capital One. The terms of the card are heavily weighted in favor of the lender, but it allowed him to establish credit.

A secured card works similarly to a regular card, except you give the lender a deposit, which is held as a guarantee for payments on any credit card purchases. The amount of the deposit sets the limit of the card. Most of them add an annual fee, in this case $34, for maintaining the card. In the eyes of credit bureaus, the secured card is treated exactly as any other credit card.

The card worked. He was very careful to only use the card to purchase things for which he had money. Opening the account with a limit of $1,000, he used it regularly for purchases from soft drinks to airline tickets, and paid off the balance each month religiously.

After just five months, he decided to buy a car. With the original credit score of 621, he would have either been denied a car loan or ended up with an interest rate of more than 9%. But in that short time, his score had gone up 110 points to 731. Instead of rejecting him, they approved the loan at a rate of 3.99%.

GET THE MOST OUT OF YOUR CREDIT CARDS

The reality is, as my intern's story illustrates, you must use credit in order to *have* credit. It's not the fact you use credit cards that causes problems; it's how you use them. Maximize the benefit of your cards by understanding what affects your credit score. Here are a few guidelines that should help you make decisions:

■ **Get the right cards.** If you have no credit at all, cards from department stores and gas companies are not the best way to get started. In fact, they might be hurting your credit score. Cards are not all created equal. To achieve the highest credit scores, you need to use the biggest cards: Visa, MasterCard, Discover, or American Express.

Department store and subprime cards—cards issued to those with substandard credit scores—carry the highest interest rates, making them the most expensive to maintain, plus they have frequent incentives to use them. If you are a shopaholic, this is a dangerous position to put yourself in. Additionally, every time you open a new card, you add a credit inquiry to your credit report, which lowers your score. Department store card limits are usually lower, which makes it more difficult to maintain a good utilization ratio, as explained later in this section. You will always be better off if you stick with the major cards.

If you don't qualify for one of those cards, consider starting with a secured card, as my intern did. You can find options at a number of sites, such as www.CardRatings.com, www.CreditCards.com, www.LowCards.com, and www.NerdWallet.com. Make sure the site you choose reports to the three big credit bureaus, and request secured cards that can be converted to regular credit cards after a year or two of on-time payments.

■ **Limit the number of cards.** When I first looked at my credit report, I realized I had a large number of cards—particularly department store cards—that just sat there. I never used them anymore. There is a ratio of how much credit limit you have to how much debt you have. Cards sitting idle don't help your numbers. Don't cancel them, however; keep making payments and stop using them until they go inactive. If you do decide to close them, don't do it all at once. Closing a large amount of credit cards could also hurt your credit.

You should have at least three lines of credit for the best scores. Any less than that, and the credit bureaus won't have enough information about your spending habits to form an accurate judgment.

Conversely, if you have more than five cards, credit bureaus will figure you have more opportunities to overextend yourself, and are more likely to lower your score. Besides, the more cards you have, the greater the chance that errors will find their way onto your credit report.

■ **Be aware of your utilization ratio.** That's a fancy term to describe how much you use your cards. More than a third of your credit score is determined by the amount of credit available to you that you don't use. The more unused available credit you have, the better your credit score will be. You should always try to keep your balance below 30 percent of a card's limit. It's even better if you can keep it below 10 percent. For example, if you have a credit limit of $10,000, you should never have more than a $1,000 balance.

This applies to each card. For example, if you have two cards, each with a limit of $10,000, and Card A has a balance of $1,000, it reflects 10 percent utilization. If Card B has a balance of $4,000, it shows a 40 percent ratio, and you need to bring it down to 30 percent or lower. There are several ways you can do this. The most obvious is to pay off $1,000 on Card B. If you don't have that much cash, however, there are other options.

First, you can ask the credit card company to increase the limit on the card. Or, complete a balance transfer from Card B to Card A, raising the lower balance and reducing the larger, keeping both within the 30 percent range.

Another possibility is to open a new card and transfer the necessary amount to the new account. Be careful with this choice: Open the account first and then initiate the transfer. If you open the card by doing the transfer, the new card may only give you a limit equal to the amount you want to transfer, which would make the utilization ratio for the new card 100 percent.

Be aware that your utilization ratio is computed even if you pay off the entire balance each month. The balance reported to the credit bureau is usually whatever amount was on your last statement; if you pay off the total balance each time you get a bill, you must still be cautious not to charge more than 30 percent of the card's limit.

■ **Don't let the card sit idle.** While using your card too much is unfavorable, it is unwise to never use them. Optimal use is to keep your card activity low and pay off the balance each month, so that you don't end up paying a ton of interest. You don't have to carry a large balance in order to use credit.

WATCH OUT FOR CREDIT
CARD COMPANY DIRTY TRICKS

In a recent interview with credit scoring expert Philip Tirone (www.philiptirone.com), I learned a startling fact: About half of the credit card companies don't report card limits accurately to credit bureaus. For example, your card carrying a limit of $1,000 may only show a $500 limit on the credit report. Even if you kept the balance at 30 percent of the limit shown on your monthly statement (below $300), that $300 will look like 60 percent on your credit report, causing your credit score to drop.

Why do they do this? According to Philip, they don't want to lose you to competition. Credit card companies target offers for new cards to people with certain credit limits. If you have a limit of $10,000, you're likely to get an offer from a different company, hoping to convince you to switch from your current card. If your limit is falsely reported as $5,000, you will not be targeted by the competition.

This practice is completely illegal, of course, but that doesn't stop it from happening, so beware. Your score will suffer. Philip shared three suggestions with me that can help correct this problem:

1. Check your credit report and confirm whether or not the limits are reported accurately. If you find an error, call the credit card company and ask them to rectify it.

2. If this doesn't work, send a letter to the credit card company, asking them to verify your limits. Don't say anything threatening or complaining. The letter should appear to be a routine check into the limits of your existing cards. Once you receive the confirmation letter, write a letter to the credit bureau requesting that it correct the error. Include a copy of the credit card company's confirmation letter, a copy of your credit card bill showing the correct credit limit, and a copy of the credit report showing the incorrect limit.

3. If neither of those work, call the credit card company again and read the riot act to customer service. Inform the representative that you are recording the call, and demand that the company report the proper limit. As a last resort, report the company to your state's Attorney General's office. The practice of incorrect credit reporting is, after all, illegal. Usually, however, you will find the problem resolved within the first two steps.

Go / No Go

Credit Repair Checklist

Do you have spending habits that need to be changed, such as eating out frequently or shopping for clothes when you don't need to?

_____ **Go**   _____ **No Go**

How many credit cards do you have? Do you have at least three?

_____ **Go**   _____ **No Go**

Do you have more than five?

_____ **Go**   _____ **No Go**

What cards do you have? How many are major credit cards? Department store cards? Gas cards? Others?

_____ **Go**   _____ **No Go**

For each card, what is your utilization ratio? What is your balance? What is your card limit?

_____ **Go**   _____ **No Go**

Are the limits on your cards reported correctly on your credit report?

_____ **Go**   _____ **No Go**

SUMMARY

- Credit repair takes time. The more negative items on your credit score, the longer it will take.

- High debt lowers your credit score, but so does no debt.

- Every time you apply for credit and a credit check is run, it lowers your credit score.

- The first step in repairing your credit is to gain control of your spending. This requires lifestyle changes.

- To establish credit, you must use credit, but you must demonstrate reliability. You cannot miss payments—ever.

- Pay off your debt. Stop charging things and find ways to reduce the amounts you owe.

- Credit cards have become necessary; get the most out of them by using them in a way that helps your credit score rather than bringing it down.

- Make sure you have the right credit cards, primarily Visa, MasterCard, Discover, or American Express. Avoid department store cards and subprime cards.

- Limit the number of cards. You should have at least three but no more than five.

- Keep your utilization ratio as low as possible. Never use more than 30 percent of the available limit on any card.

- Check your credit report to make sure your card limits have been reported accurately.

WEEK 5

LAND NAVIGATION CERTIFICATION— IDENTIFY YOUR GOALS

"This isn't good."

Those were not words I wanted to hear, and coming from an experienced Navy SEAL, they were especially ominous. We were in the middle of Baghdad, far outside our normal operating area, in the middle of the night.

One of my squad's primary assignments was to protect a high-ranking Iraqi official. Any time he needed, or wanted, to go somewhere, we were to escort him. This night in particular, he was to make an appearance at a bank that had been attacked. We received

the call at two o'clock one morning. From a dead sleep, we had twenty minutes to be ready and out the gate.

Setting out to our unknown destination was the first time I had ventured into the middle of Baghdad. Not only did we not know where we were going, but also as we drove along, I noticed civilians along the street wearing black ski masks, armed with AK-47s.

Our training prepared us to fight an enemy, but in this situation, there was no way of knowing who was a friend and who was a foe. Only if they started shooting would we know they were the enemy. Many were probably Iraqi guardsmen, who often wore masks to protect their identity, but we had no way of knowing for sure and all we could do was hope for the best.

Eventually reaching our objective, we drove past the bank and turned left into a cul-de-sac. From there we made another left-hand turn, into an alley, hoping to then turn our vehicles around for the return trip. But the alley was nothing more than a dead end, too narrow for turning. In the pitch dark of early morning, backing out required us to alight from the Humvee.

It was at this point that the Navy SEAL made his ominous comment: "This isn't good."

Nervous enough already, I didn't need him to tell me that, but he didn't stop there. "This isn't good. We need at least two hundred guys where we are right now." We had close to fifty, including the SEALs.

Fortunately, nothing terrible happened. Eventually making our way out of the alley, we completed the mission and headed back to base. This experience impressed on me the importance of knowing where you're going. I never wanted to feel that way again.

If you feel that your financial situation is hopeless, it's probably because you have not figured out exactly where you want to go. Set goals to define your mission, and then develop the skills and discipline to accomplish them. Without a clear understanding of your destination, you will not only have a tough time getting to where you need to be, you will not enjoy the trip.

Every mission has a purpose. When you made the decision to become a Soldier of Finance, you must have had at least one or two goals in mind. Perhaps you want to save for retirement. Maybe you want to start a business or pay off student loans, or fund your kids' education. Whatever the goal, it needs to be clear and detailed. You don't want to head off into the financial war zone without knowing where you're going. Define and refine your goals, then move toward fulfilling them.

DEFINE YOUR MISSION OBJECTIVES

Goals are closely connected to orders. Military missions always start with a basic objective in mind. This objective helps to define the type of operation you need to plan in order to accomplish them.

Your goals should be well thought out and detailed. Setting both short-term and long-term goals is imperative. These include:

- Lifetime goals

- 3-year goals

- 1-year goals

- 90-day goals

These goals define your overall financial missions; you will likely have several goals in each category. Begin with lifetime goals and set shorter-term goals to build toward them. Take your time as you think these through. Don't forget that lifetime goals involve your Battle Buddy, so be sure to set aside time to talk through them together. Be specific. For example, "I want to get out of debt" and "I want to make a million dollars" are good ideas, but they are not detailed. They are more of a dream than a specific mission. You will need to think through the details and realistically set goals that you can reach. Instead of saying, "I want to make a lot of money," determine specific amounts and build a plan to attain them, based on where you are now and what stands in the way of your goal. It might look something like this:

- **Lifetime goal:** Retire at 45 with a minimum of $1 million in my portfolio.

- **3-year goal:** Have $100,000 set aside for investments that can create passive income for retirement.

- **1-year goal:** Pay $18,000 off my credit card debt.

- **90-day goal:** Stop eating out more than once a week and put aside the money I save for future investment.

Your goals may change as time goes on, but if you don't have something specific, they will never happen. If you don't know where you're going, you'll never get there.

WARRIOR TASK
Mission Objectives

List your specific goals in the following areas:

Lifetime goal: _____

3-year goal: _____

1-year goal: _____

90-day goal: _____

OP ORDERS: HOW TO ACHIEVE YOUR MISSION

Now that you've set specific goals, plan the details of how to attack each one in turn. Military Operation Orders, or "Op Orders" for short, are directives summarizing the intent of the operation. They outline exactly what needs to be done in order to achieve the desired result. In other words, Op Orders are the plan for achieving goals. They are designed to make sure everyone involved is absolutely clear on expectations, roles, and assignments.

The only real difference for a Soldier of Finance is that you give your own orders, based on your mission and your goals.

Complete an Op Order for each goal. Writing things down is an important part of organizing your plan and sticking with it. Something about the act of putting ink on paper increases your belief in the goals and your motivation to achieve them. You will find inspiration by periodically reviewing what you have planned and written, especially as you see the progress you have made.

Yes, you can plan it in your head, but the process of writing forces you to think things through more thoroughly than you are otherwise likely to. It will also help you to remember the plan and commitments involved. Resist the temptation to sit at your computer and type them out. You want a handwritten hard copy.

Your Op Order includes several steps:

- **Step 1. Name the mission.** Think of each financial goal as a separate mission. I recommend that you give the operation a name. Big military operations always have a grandiose name to instill confidence in personnel. In my lifetime, the best known have been Operation Desert Storm, Operation Desert Shield, and Operation Iraqi Freedom. Giving your goals a code name will help you stay focused and add a little fun to the process.

  The name can be anything that helps you identify the goal. Operation Student Loan would be a typical code name for your attack on your college debt. Paying off credit cards could be Operation Discover Freedom or Operation Visa Revocation. Whatever name you decide to use, write it in the first line of your Op Order.

- **Step 2. Define the mission.** Naming the mission is one step in defining it; it also needs to be clarified in detail. Decide exactly what you want to accomplish. Everything previously discussed about the specific details of setting goals applies here. Do not be vague. You will have to follow this plan, so think it through.

  Don't make the mission so complicated that you can't keep track of it. Make it something simple, like "Pay off the $5,000 balance on my Visa card." Referring to the information in your SIT Report will help determine if your Visa card is the ideal debt to tackle first. If it is, then tackle it first. Rank the debts listed in your SIT Report by priority and write the first priority in the second line of your Op Order form.

■ **Step 3. Define the timeline for the mission.** Give your mission a specific time frame. Be realistic about what you can do. If you can put aside an extra $500 a month to tackle your Visa card, then you can assume a 10-month duration for the mission. The exact time will not be quite as simple to figure due to interest calculations, but if you can't figure that out, at least set a general timeline. With a date set, you can determine what you need to do on a weekly and monthly basis in order to stay on track.

■ **Step 4. Analyze the situation.** Every mission will be different. Once you know what you want to accomplish, you can analyze your resources and the obstacles you face; essentially, compare your strengths and weaknesses.

Do you have a stable paycheck? Do you have things you could sell to help pay off a debt? Do you have a burning desire to eliminate this debt? These are all strengths. You need to acknowledge your weaknesses as well. They include anything that will negatively impact your ability to reach your goal. If you have no savings, that is a weakness. If you are a shopaholic, that's a weakness. If you are unemployed, that is definitely a weakness you will need to address in your mission planning.

In fact, if a weakness is big enough to derail the whole operation, consider placing one mission on hold while you deal with the other. Mission Visa Reduction might have to wait for Mission Get a Job.

Once you have assessed your resources, get creative. Let your imagination run wild. What could you do to earn extra money? What can you sell? Do you have any talents that you can use to make additional income? What expenses can you eliminate from your daily life that will leave more money for your goals? Do you really need a gym membership? You could exercise by running around the park and save that amount in your monthly budget. Opportunities are everywhere if you start looking around.

Finally, consider threats to your plan. I like to think of these as the obstacles you must overcome, or the enemies you must defeat, in order to reach your goal. It will be very difficult to completely eliminate credit card debt if you are still charging purchases. If you don't have any money in savings and rely solely on your plastic in the event of an emergency, a sudden car breakdown or a medical crisis could cause you some serious problems in reaching your goal.

You might not be able to do anything about some of these problems, but you should at least be aware of them. And if you *can* do something about them, then add that to your overall plan.

- **Step 5. Plan your attack.** Once you have completely analyzed the situation at hand and fully understand the importance and details of your goal, it's time to determine exactly how you will progress toward it. This is where minute details come into play, and they cannot be discounted.

  A goal is made up of many smaller segments; it is important to develop a plan of attack in small increments. If your mission of paying off a $5,000 balance in ten months requires that you make an additional payment each month of $500 to bring the principal down, and you get a weekly paycheck, you must plan to set aside $125 from each check in order to meet your goal. Details become important subgoals in the bigger picture.

  I cannot stress how important such planning is. That night in Baghdad, I desperately wished that someone had done a little more planning, so we at least knew where we were and how to get help if we needed it. We were fortunate that nothing bad happened, and you can't predict everything. What you *can* do is plan as much as possible to minimize the surprises. Success depends on knowing where you're going. As Yogi Berra said, *"If you don't know where you are going, you will wind up somewhere else."*

W A R R I O R   T A S K
Op Order

Select your first goal and create an Op Order for accomplishing it. Repeat this process for each goal that you have right now.

1. Mission Name: _____

2. Define the Mission: _____

3. Define the Timeline of the Mission: _____

   _____

   _____

4. Analyze the Situation: _____

   a. Strengths: _____

      _____

      _____

   b. Weaknesses: _____

      _____

      _____

5. Plan Your Attack: _____

   a. _____

(Continues on next page)

b. _____

c. _____

d. _____

Go / No Go

Goal Setting

Have you set lifetime goals?

_____ **Go**   _____ **No Go**

Have you set 3-year goals?

_____ **Go**   _____ **No Go**

Have you set 1-year goals?

_____ **Go**   _____ **No Go**

Have you set 90-day goals?

_____ **Go**   _____ **No Go**

Do you have completed Op Orders for each goal?

_____ **Go**   _____ **No Go**

SUMMARY

- Goals and objectives define the type of operation you need to plan.

- Define your mission objective by setting specific short-term and long-term goals.

- Goals should be written down as your personal Operation Orders.

  - Give the specific mission a name.

  - Define what the mission is, such as "Pay off Visa card."

  - Set timelines for the mission.

  - Analyze the situation, including your resources and the obstacles you face.

  - Devise a detailed plan of how you will accomplish your goal.

PART THREE

CAMPAIGN PHASE (WEEKS 6–12)

Phase Two is designed to launch your attack on your financial enemies. You have identified what needs to happen and have determined a plan of attack; the following step is to take action. This involves Tactical Budgeting and familiarization with the weapons of investment at your disposal.

By the end of the Campaign Phase, you will see measurable progress toward financial stability and enduring wealth.

Are you ready to take action?

WEEK 6

ACCOMPLISHING GOALS— FROM CHAOS TO PRECISION

They treated us like cattle. Literally. The day we left Reception, we knew we were headed to Basic Training, but in all honesty, not one of us really knew where we were going. The trip should have given us a clue.

Reception took a little over a week. We finished the required paperwork and went into a kind of holding pattern until a slot opened up for us in Basic. Notice finally came to get our gear and head out the door; we were heading down range. Dragging along our two duffel bags and rucksacks packed to the brim, we stumbled out the door to load up for the ten-minute drive.

To say they treated us like cattle would not paint an accurate impression. Cattle would have been allowed more room. We stepped into what we called cattle cars, basically big boxes on wheels, pulled by a truck. I wouldn't be surprised to learn that they actually did haul cattle at one time.

I don't know how those things were considered legal. Loaded down with gear, we crammed in like sardines until we literally could not move. All I could think was how much I wanted the doors to open so I could breathe again.

Ten minutes seemed like eternity, but we finally arrived. Before we stepped off the cattle cars, I could hear drill sergeants screaming and yelling. Mad chaos is the only description that can do the scene justice. New recruits stumbled from the cars in confusion and ran off in the wrong direction, abruptly changing direction when a drill sergeant screamed at them.

Twelve drill sergeants, a first sergeant, a lieutenant, and a captain all did their best to add to the pandemonium. If I hadn't been trapped in the chaos myself, it would have been hilarious. One drill sergeant ordered a soldier to hold his duffel bag above his head. He had laundry detergent in his duffel bag, and, somewhere in the mayhem, it broke open and ran down over his head. The drill sergeant screamed at him for messing up his formation area.

Starting from that scene of total confusion, we figured out how to function as soldiers. Our drill sergeants, who that morning took just a few minutes to have us all standing at stiff attention in perfect lines, molded ignorant civilians into precision soldiers. We learned that we could handle the pressure. We discovered that we had what it takes to deal with the pressure. We learned how to work together as a team to accomplish virtually anything. The training set before us a clear vision of what a soldier is and pushed us toward that goal.

INTO ACTION

What a contrast between that first day, when none of us had any idea where we were supposed to stand, and my arrival in Iraq as a staff sergeant (E-6), responsible for a squad of nine other guys. Beyond my comfort zone, I at least knew what was expected of me, and I was trained to handle the responsibility.

At Basic, the only goal we had as we stepped off the cattle cars was to become a soldier. By the time I arrived in Iraq, I understood that a mission, *any mission*, had to be a lot more specific if I wanted it to succeed. In Iraq, we never went anywhere without specific goals in mind. And not once did the chaos of combat overwhelm us.

My baptism under fire served to prove how important it is to know where you're going. Stationed in Baghdad, my squad had orders to conduct regular patrols along a route known for a lot of activity. To ensure I knew where we were going, I rode with a "Regular Army" veteran team the day before our turn. I expected action of some kind, but fortunately nothing happened that day, enabling me to learn the lay of the land. When our turn came the following day, I had the confidence of knowing where we were.

Good thing I did. Within an hour of beginning our patrol, we came across a possible IED (Improvised Explosive Device). Thanks to the training endured back at Basic, we knew exactly how to handle the situation. Without chaos or confusion, the area was cordoned off and EOD (Explosive Ordnance Disposal) called in.

Later in the mission, I had my first experience of being under fire: Standing and talking with one of the other men, I suddenly heard a buzzing sound, like a large horsefly whizzing by. A sniper had taken aim at us. I'd be lying if I said my adrenaline levels weren't elevated, but our training had prepared us for this.

Surprisingly, my initial thought was not to dive for cover. In fact, I don't believe anyone reacted this way. The first thing that went through my mind was, "What an idiot! We have tanks here; keep shooting and we'll pinpoint your location and blow you up."

This all happened within the first hour. When we finally got under way again, we came across a bus full of prisoners being transported to Abu Ghraib prison. The bus had been lit up by automatic fire; its entire side was riddled with bullet holes, and the bloodied and mutilated bodies of dead and wounded Iraqis surrounded the vehicle.

The first at the scene were the crew I had ridden with the day earlier. I distinctly recall standing over a wounded Iraqi; his breathing pattern clearly indicated that he would not make it. He didn't speak English, so all I could offer was a nod as I told him, "It's gonna be okay."

The wounded were medivaced out on a chopper as bullets from snipers buzzed by. People ran back and forth, shouting. It was three hours of chaos. Not the kind of chaos we experienced the day we got off the cattle cars; here, everyone knew what he was supposed to do. In spite of the urgency to move quickly and guard against further attacks, there was no panic. We all knew our jobs and we did them.

The situation wound down when we received an order to escort another bus. This time, my confidence waned a little; we were heading into an area I wasn't familiar with, without time to prepare. Not only were we heading deeper into the Red Zone—where help was 20 minutes away—we only had three trucks. Patrols like that usually had six. Traveling into known dangerous territory at half strength, without knowing exactly where we were, was extremely unappealing. Yet, we made it through and returned to base without further incident. Seems the day had been exciting enough already.

EXECUTE THE MISSION

You've now completed a significant amount of training, just as we soldiers did. You've taken the time to plan your mission, breaking it down into manageable elements. The time has come to execute your mission, that is, to begin moving in the direction of your specific, detailed goals. No matter how much you want to succeed, nothing happens until you begin to act. Unlike missions in Iraq, where we were ordered into a situation and forced to execute in order to stay alive, you will have to make the choice to execute this mission on your own.

The first few days will be easy. Your enthusiasm will carry you for a while, but as the daily grind of life begins to set in, your interest will be diverted to other, more pleasant things. That's to be expected; it happens to everyone. When you talk to a recruiter, you will be excited by his appeal to your patriotism, but six weeks into training, the last thing you'll have on your mind is home and country. All you'll think about is how much your muscles hurt. That's when you need techniques for keeping yourself motivated. Fortunately, there are a few things you can do:

- **Keep your goals fresh in mind by reviewing them regularly.** Ask your Battle Buddy to help you with this—that's your Buddy's role. Share your fears and worries and be honest when you're struggling. Talking it out will help.

- **Automate your plan as much as possible.** Set up automatic payments and establish an automatic savings plan, with money taken directly from your paycheck. Stay on track; avoid the temptation of spending before you've taken care of your Op Order.

- **Make significant changes to your lifestyle.** Run your air conditioner less, walk instead of driving when you're just going around the corner, and eat at home more often. Many of these suggestions will appear in the Strengths section of your mission analysis as we saw in Chapter 7. The sooner you implement them, the sooner you will benefit.

- **Look for new opportunities to make changes that will help you reach your goal sooner.** Possibilities present themselves all the time. For example, I enjoy reading. While overseas, we had moments of downtime and nowhere to go; being goal-oriented, I used the time to achieve the personal goal of reading every John Grisham book in print. Back then, that meant getting through more than a dozen full-length novels. Surprisingly, I finished that goal much sooner than expected, leaving me to find another goal to work toward.

It occurred to me that I could continue reading *and* work toward a life goal at the same time. I knew I wanted to become a Certified Financial Planner (CFP), and one of the stepping-stones along the way was to become a Chartered Retirement Planning Counselor (CRPC). I had heard there was a class I could take online, so that became my new goal.

I called home and had my office send me the study materials. In just a few months, at 1:00 AM Baghdad time, I took the test to become a CRPC.

TWENTY-ONE DAYS TO CHANGE

A lot of the problems we experience with self-discipline are essentially a matter of bad habits. Take a look at your credit report; from the information contained there, you will be able to identify some of your bad financial habits. Bad habits are very difficult to break, but they're not impossible. Just don't expect to change them overnight. As Mark Twain said, *"Habit is habit, and not to be flung out of the window by any man, but coaxed downstairs a step at a time."*

The positive side of this is that a good habit is just as difficult to change as a bad one. The trick is identifying your bad spending habits and replacing them with good ones. Aristotle said, *"We are what we repeatedly do. Excellence, then, is not an act, but a habit."*

It is often said that you can change a habit in twenty-one days. That number can vary, depending on how ingrained the habit is and what you replace it with, but in general, it's a good rule of thumb. Pick a bad financial habit and focus on it for twenty-one days. That's just three weeks.

Change one habit at a time. Don't try to take on more than you can handle and set yourself up to fail. Realistically, one habit will take all of your focus. The habit might be as simple as deciding that you will stop eating out every day. Perhaps you spend too much on credit. Decide that you will not add to your credit card debt for twenty-one days. Do you go clothes shopping daily? Perhaps you need to curtail that habit. Determine what you spend too much money on and focus on those things, one at a time.

Here are some basic guidelines that will help change your habits:

- **Write it down.** You are setting a short-term goal in every sense of the word, so treat it the same way you treated the goals in your Op Orders in Chapter 7. Identify the habit you want to change in detail. To help clarify your goals, write down exactly why you want to change that habit. Give yourself the strongest motivation you can.

- **Plan a support system.** No military operation should ever be executed without utilizing every available resource. Discuss the habit with your Battle Buddy and be certain you will be supported and held accountable.

- **If you miss a day or two, don't beat yourself up.** Simply start again, right away. Persistence is the key to establishing new habits. Keep at it and you *will* succeed.

WARRIOR TASK
Breaking Habits

1. Select one bad financial habit, such as eating out every day.

2. Focus on that habit for twenty-one days.

3. Write down what the habit is and devise a plan for changing it.

4. Get your Battle Buddy to check with you periodically to keep you accountable.

DEALING WITH SETBACKS

No matter how much you plan, there will be things you can't predict ahead of time. When I went to Basic, I believed I would finish without a problem, and continue on to collect my GI benefits and go to college. Once I settled into the routine, I felt fairly comfortable with the whole process. I knew I could handle the training and I managed to stay (mostly) unnoticed by the drill sergeants and didn't get smoked too often.

Sometime in the first month or so, I began to feel pain in my legs. It started as shin splints that got worse every day. Eventually it escalated to the point where I could not walk without pain.

I was determined to stick it out. Basic lasts for three months; if you drop out due to an injury, you have to start over from the beginning. The last thing I wanted to do was repeat my training. I kept my mouth shut and endured the pain, until finally I couldn't take it anymore. We were on a five-mile run and somewhere in the second or third mile, I knew something wasn't right. It was more than shin splints and I had to stop.

Of course, the first sergeant was on me in an instant, screaming every name in the book.

I tried to defend myself, "First Sergeant, something ain't right."

"Oh, you're a doctor, now? Now you're telling me how everything is?"

But I couldn't run anymore. I ended up on the back of a five-ton truck with everyone else who dropped out—not exactly the place I wanted to be. As soon as we got back, I went to sick call to see a doctor, who diagnosed a stress fracture in my leg. I had been running for weeks on a broken leg. I limped out of there with a full-leg cast.

Devastated, I was only five weeks shy of finishing Basic and certainly didn't want to repeat the first seven weeks. I reported to my drill sergeant, who was a little surprised when he noticed my cast; he certainly wouldn't say the words, but I suspected he felt bad for me. After looking at it for a minute, he said, "You know, you could go as far as you can with the cast. That will increase your chances of not having to go back to the beginning."

The remaining five weeks involved many tasks I could do. It would be challenging, but it was worth taking a shot. A lot of the training required firing different weapons in order to qualify for them. I didn't need to run to fire a grenade launcher; I just had to get to the firing range.

I gained a lot of respect from my drill sergeants when they saw me hobble up to the range on two crutches, dragging my cast. Showing up for field maneuvers, lugging an M-16 along with my crutches, I completed every element of the training that my cast allowed, and it worked.

With this newfound respect, I got the okay to sit out the beginning of the following training cycle to allow my leg to heal, and was able to pick up where I left off and complete the training. Basic and Advanced Individual Training took six months instead of three, but I made it through and earned a great deal of respect in the process.

Not everything will go as planned, but setbacks are not an excuse to give up on your plans or goals. The setback in Basic Training affected more than just my time there. By the time I finally healed and returned home, I had missed the opportunity to enroll in a full load of classes. I managed to take some courses at Santa Monica Community College that summer, and I avoided parking tickets this time! After that first semester, I moved back to the Midwest and finished my associate's degree at John A. Logan College in southern Illinois. It took me four years to finish a two-year degree. But I got the degree and I was that much closer to my life goals.

REVIEW THE MISSION

During our pre-deployment training at Fort Dix, New Jersey, we were put through a ton of different exercises and drills. Many times the instructors set us up for failure, not for their own satisfaction (although it definitely felt that way at times), but to see how we would react under pressure.

Our squad failed miserably at the onset. It would have been easy to be hard on ourselves, but after each mission we would do a recap of all the items that went well and all the items that needed to be improved. This was called the After Action Report (AAR).

The concept of an After Action Report is to analyze what happened, what worked, and how the next operation can be improved. In both the military and business worlds, such analysis is practiced frequently and consistently.

As a Soldier of Finance, frequent AARs give you the opportunity to constantly improve your financial strategy. If something is not working, adjustments can be made. Flexibility plays an important role in success.

WARRIOR TASK
After Action Report

1. Mission Name: _____

2. Analysis:

   a.   Goals that were met: _____

   b.   Goals that were not met: _____

   c.   Reason for failure: _____

   d.   Changes: _____

Go / No Go

Accomplishing Your Goals

Are you ready to begin working toward the first goal on your list?

_____ **Go**   _____ **No Go**

Have you developed a plan for achieving your goals?

_____ **Go**   _____ **No Go**

Have you identified changes you can make in your lifestyle that will help you accomplish your goals? What are they?

_____ **Go**   _____ **No Go**

Do you need to learn specific skills or information to accomplish your goals?

_____ **Go**   _____ **No Go**

Have you identified bad habits that are keeping you from your goals?

_____ **Go**   _____ **No Go**

SUMMARY

- No matter how much you want to succeed, nothing happens until you begin to act.

- Keep your goals fresh in mind by reviewing them regularly.

- Automate your plan as much as possible. Set up automatic payments. Arrange to have savings taken directly out of your paycheck.

- Make changes in your lifestyle to provide more money to accomplish your goals, such as eating at home more often.

- Watch for opportunities to reach your goal sooner. For example, if you have dead time in your schedule, use it to read material that will help you grow toward your goals.

- Identify bad financial habits and work toward changing them, one habit at a time. Write down what the habit is. Plan a support system to help you and keep you accountable. If you miss a day, start again right away.

- Everyone meets with setbacks. Do not let a setback stop you from persevering. Adjust as you need to and persevere toward your goals.

WEEK 7

DESTROYING THE ENEMY— PAYING OFF DEBT

Debt is your enemy. When you want something more than anything in the world and the only way you can get it is to set up a payment schedule, debt seems like your friend. But it's not. Debt is your enemy. It robs you of the resources to invest. Fortunately, I learned that lesson through a 1998 champagne-colored four-door Chevy Lumina sedan.

What I wanted more than anything was a sexy car. Ideally, that would be a BMW sports car. When I first moved back to Illinois to attend junior college, I got as close as I could with my budget—a red '96 Pontiac Grand Am. It was the first car I was responsible for paying for.

Fortunately, my grandmother paid it off as a graduation gift. I was supporting myself at the time, with the help of the National Guard, and I didn't need a $350 a month car payment. But I still dreamed. A Grand Am was nice, but hardly what I pictured myself driving when I imagined my future.

Unfortunately, when people fantasize about sports cars, they fail to recognize the reality of what it will cost them. The truth came to me in my Finance 361 class. The professor asked one question, followed by the statement that changed my life to the tune of more than $2 million.

"How many of you plan to buy a new car every three to five years?" he asked. "Raise your hand." The image of me wearing sunglasses behind the wheel of a BMW flashed through my mind, and my hand went up. Over half the class raised their hands with me. Then the professor made a statement that has stuck with me ever since:

"Enjoy making your car payments for the rest of your life while I take my family to Europe on vacation whenever I want."

He allowed the comment to settle before explaining it. For the first time, I began to understand the concept of the time value of money and compounding interest. I realized what the debt incurred in buying a new car would rob me of in the future. Because I put money into a Roth IRA and a 401(k) instead of a car payment, my money began building early.

A few years into my career, my grandmother passed away. Among the things I inherited was that Chevy Lumina. My wife and I called it "the Lu." It was fully paid for with only 11,000 miles, in excellent condition, clean and reliable. Though it was six years old, it looked brand new. But it was a grandma car. Dreams of a BMW didn't include anything with four doors.

Before college, I would have sold the Grand Am, sold the Lumina, and used the money on a down payment for the car I really wanted. But now, instead of an image of a BMW flashing through my mind, I saw car payments robbing me of the benefits of compounding investments. My thinking had changed.

I sold the Grand Am and drove the Lu. With no car payment to worry about, I started putting money into a Roth IRA until I maxed it out. Then I started a 401(k). I was able to put a minimum of $400 a month into investments, often more.

What does that mean in the long run? I used a Roth IRA savings calculator to project my earnings. With a $5,000 investment each year, assuming a 10% annual return, by the time I reach 65, I will have $2,683,185. If you think that's too optimistic, then what if I'm off by 50 percent? I still will have well over $1.4 million!

Suppose I had opted to sell the Lu and buy a BMW. Not only would my money have gone into payments every month and been gone, but I would not have started serious investing until three years later. Using the same calculations, I would only have $2,002,239, a difference of $680,946 for simply delaying three years before I started investing.

As significant as that difference is, I also realize that if I had not started at age 24, I would very likely not have started at 27 either. That is typical of most people. Ultimately, a sports car would have translated into a debt. A few years later, most likely before that debt was paid off, I would have traded the car in for a newer model and perpetuated the debt. When I began to understand that debt was my enemy, the car didn't seem so exciting anymore. It cost far more than I was willing to pay in the long run.

Whenever I think of that car, I recognize that it was a turning point in my life. I call it the "Lu Trap." On the surface, it appeared to be a choice between driving a Lumina and driving a BMW. In reality, it was a choice between paying interest to a creditor or collecting interest from investments. The Lu Trap enabled me to clearly see that I would not have acquired a sports car; I would have acquired a debt.

Understand the importance of the Lu Trap in your life. If you have debt, you absolutely have to get rid of it and begin investing . . . The sooner the better. Every year you delay costs you many thousands of dollars, perhaps millions.

FIELD ARTILLERY: MATCHING
THE CANNON TO THE OBJECTIVE

Any guy who says he doesn't enjoy blowing stuff up is probably lying (that's true for a few women I know, too, but it's a universal truth for men). As kids we're fascinated with firecrackers. As adults we can join the Army and play with real guns and grenades. I took it a step further.

When I moved from California back to Illinois, the closest infantry unit was more than three hours from my home. Instead of making the long drive for weekend drills, I transferred to a closer field artillery unit. I didn't do that just so I could blow stuff up, of course, but since I was there, why not enjoy it?

The mission of infantry is to be on the front lines, engaging the enemy directly. As a member of the field artillery, I took on a different mission: to destroy, neutralize, or suppress the enemy by cannon fire from afar . . . otherwise known as blowing stuff up.

We had a variety of ammunition to choose from. High Explosive rounds (HE) and Rocket Assisted Projectiles (RAP) were lethal anti-infantry weapons. White Phosphorus rounds (WP) could start fires to burn targets and create smoke for concealment. Illumination rounds fired a flare into the air with a parachute attached. There were rounds designed to scatter land mines, both anti-personnel (ADAMS) and anti-armor (RAAMS). Other rounds exploded in the air and scattered small-shaped charge explosives that can penetrate two inches of steel. The type of shell selected depended on the target and objective.

AMMUNITION FOR TARGETING DEBT

When it comes to taking on your debt load, be as methodical and deliberate as if you were firing a howitzer. A variety of strategies are available to you. Which type of ammunition you employ depends on the size and type of debt you have accumulated. It also depends on your personality and which approach you will best implement and stick with. Your SIT Report has all the necessary information to help you.

In the following, I've identified each strategy with a type of ammunition. Your goal is the elimination of your debt. Select the right shell and prepare to start firing:

■ **HI Round (High Interest)—The Mathematical Formula.** People who like numbers and formulas (I know there are some of you out there) often prefer this method, because it makes the most sense mathematically. List all of your debts in order, with the highest rate of interest at the top. While making the minimum payment on each debt, focus extra attention on the first debt on the list. Put as much extra as you can on that debt each month until it is paid off.

Once that debt is gone, focus on the next one, moving gradually down the list. As you pay off a debt, take the money from that payment and apply it to the next debt, rather than spending it on something else. The further down the list you go, the faster the debts will disappear.

Over the long run, this plan will save you the most money because you're eliminating the most expensive debts first. It's simple math.

- **IM Round (Increasing Momentum)—The Snowball.** This is a popular method introduced by radio host and author Dave Ramsey. List all of your debts in order of the remaining balance, beginning with the smallest and ending with the largest. Like the High Interest plan, you pay the minimum on each debt, but in this case you put as much extra as possible on the smallest debt. By paying the smallest off first, you build confidence each time you cross something off your list.

   I've been a big fan of Ramsey's snowball method for years and often suggest it to people trying to overcome piles of debt. There are critics who wonder why people should pay off a smaller amount that has a low interest rate, when they have a larger balance with a higher rate that will ultimately cost them more.

   But experience has shown me that many people have difficulty jumping into the big debts without feeling some sense of accomplishment first. The High Interest method requires a certain level of self-discipline, and if most people had that, they probably would not be in serious debt to begin with. By taking baby steps and getting used to checking debts off your list, you're likely to get more excited about the bigger targets.

- **HE Round (High Emotion)—The Debt Tsunami.** Proposed by Soldier of Finance Adam Baker, who coined the term "Debt Tsunami," this plan makes one aware of the emotional impact of certain debts. This method taps into a true hatred or vengeance you might feel toward certain debts, and uses that energy as incentive to make progress.

First, prioritize your debts with the smallest balance first, including the interest rate with each entry.

The next step is what gives the High Emotion attack its impact and uniqueness. After you've listed all of your debts, close your eyes and visualize each item on the list. Which one weighs on you the most? Which obligation ignites a fire inside you so voracious that you will do anything to eliminate that debt? Open your eyes and put a big "X" next to that debt. You've identified your first target.

Repeat the process until you've rearranged the list according to the emotional impact the debts have on you.

The beauty of the High Emotion approach is that if you're in really hard financial times and creditors are calling several times a day, you can get the biggest monkey off your back first. It's the old principle of the squeaky wheel getting the grease. When you wipe out the debt (and the collector) that is hounding you the most, you can breathe that little bit easier and focus on the next target.

(To learn more about Baker's Debt Tsunami method, go to http://manvsdebt.com/debt-tsunami-the-ultimate-method -for-paying-off-debt.)

- **SB Round (Short Burst)—The Tabata Method.** When I was serving overseas, a buddy of mine introduced me to one of the toughest workout programs I've experienced: Crossfit. It remains my primary workout program today. To demonstrate how tough it is, the program's mascot is called Pukie the Clown. Suffice to say, I've met the mascot a few times following some workouts.

  A significant element of the Crossfit regimen is Tabata, a variation of high-intensity interval training. The idea is to alternate short bursts of high-intensity exercise with brief periods of rest.

Tabata is one of the most efficient and intense workouts I have ever put my body through. Ironically, it's also one of the shortest workout regimens. Each workout lasts four minutes.

To commence a Tabata workout, you choose an exercise. If you select push-ups, for example, you set a limit of twenty seconds. During that time, you do as many push-ups as you can. Then you rest for ten seconds. Immediately after that, you do as many more push-ups as you can for twenty seconds, followed by another ten-second rest. Repeat the process for four minutes.

What makes Tabata so effective is the concept that your body can only perform at high intensity for so long before it starts to wear down. The intervals of rest enable you to cram a lot of high-intensity exercise into a very short time, allowing enough recovery to continue to the next round.

Similarly, if you try to attack too much debt too fast, you run the risk of burning out. By applying the Tabata method, you can allow yourself breaks from the stress of hitting a debt hard. It works this way: Let's say your mission is Operation Discover. You have a balance of $10,000 on a Discover card that you maxed out when you were in college. Planning your attack on debt, you've identified this card as your first target.

To prevent early burnout, use the Tabata ratio of 2 to 1, focusing for two months and then taking a one-month rest. Make double payments for the first two months to knock a substantial amount off the principal. After hitting it hard for two months, take a month where you pay only the regular payment. Then go back to double payments for two more months. Keep repeating that cycle until the debt is eliminated.

Of course, if you aren't burned out and are able to keep making double payments every month, go for it. Be flexible and adjust to the terrain.

Operation Motherhood

Jaime Tardy, who was expecting her first child, had a very simple objective: pay off debt so that she could be a stay-at-home mom. She had two major enemies. The first was a sizable total debt, more than $70,000, including $19,000 owed on her brand-new car, two student loans totaling more than $26,000, and a sizable home equity loan. The second was the fact that her income of $100,000 a year made up 76 percent of her family's household income. She couldn't just quit while the $70,000 hung over them.

Jaime had the tenacity of a true Soldier of Finance. Her desire to be a full-time mom drove her to take on the challenge. Her Battle Buddy, her husband, fully supported her and joined in the effort.

The first objective was to tackle their debt. To do that, Jaime made a huge and difficult decision. She traded in her two-month-old Civic, which she loved. In its place, she got an eight-year-old, reliable SUV. Because the Civic was so new, she was not able to get anywhere near what she paid for it, but that one decision dropped their debt by more than $10,000, a 15 percent reduction in one move. The change also freed up $185 every month that Jaime applied to other debt.

The next phase of the mission was even tougher. They started selling stuff that had cluttered their lives for a long time. Her husband had a Jeep CJ7 with 36-inch tires, and like any Jeep enthusiast, he loved "his baby." He had spent many hours working on it. But he supported Operation Motherhood as the highest priority, so he sold his Jeep. That knocked another $5,000 off the debt.

Jaime and her husband started selling everything they didn't need, hosting not one, but three yard sales in a single summer, supplemented by a variety of *Craigslist* postings. Out the door went a kayak, a wine rack, a weight bench, and a host of other things. They cleaned out every closet and sold random things on eBay. In the process, they discovered that they had always been wrong when they thought of themselves as "minimalists." They had way too much stuff they didn't need.

The next step got down to good old-fashioned work. Jaime took on as many extra hours as she could, often traveling away from home. She put in 70 hours a week until her seventh month of pregnancy, when she dropped back to 40 hours. Her husband, a musician by trade, took on graphic design projects that he worked on in the evenings and weekends.

Restaurants became a part of their past as they kept to a strict $300-a-month grocery budget. They canceled their cable television, lowered their cell phone plans, and put themselves on a minimal allowance of $25 each for spending money each month. These were all great sacrifices for them, but the point is that the debt they targeted and the mission goals they set quickly became practical reality. They rapidly paid off the Cherokee SUV and the smaller of the two student loans. Then they took on the huge home equity loan. They often felt they weren't making any headway, but one day that loan was gone. That left only the larger student loan.

At that point, Jaime and her husband reassessed their situation and decided they needed to make a change in their priorities. Since they really didn't know what to expect with the delivery and bringing a new baby home, they decided to delay paying off the last loan while they prepared for any unexpected events. They opened a savings account and started dumping as much money into it as they could, eventually building up a reserve of $23,000.

Just four months after the baby was born, Jaime used much of her "what if" money to pay off the other student loan. At that point, because of their simpler lifestyle and less expensive habits, Jaime was able to quit her job completely and be a full-time stay-at-home mom. Mission accomplished.

You can read more about Jaime on her blog www.eventual millionaire.com.

DON'T BE CONTENT WITH DEBT

One of the biggest obstacles preventing many Americans from achieving financial independence is contentment, or rather a lack of contentment. Most people are content with high debt, as long as it contributes to their lack of contentment with the luxuries in their lives. Many want to drive a new car, own a big house, wear designer clothes, and have all the latest technological gizmos.

The truth is, most of us don't *need* half of what we go into debt to buy. And all of those comforts ultimately load us down with so much debt that they undermine happiness by adding worry every month about future security and our ability to make payments and keeping us enslaved to debt long into retirement years.

Early in my career, a man came into my office. He had just come into some money and wanted to invest it. Naturally, we discussed possible investment vehicles, but in the typical course of discussion with any new client, I try to find out as much about his financial habits as I can, in order to better handle the account.

My routine questions include these: Do you have a 401(k)? Do you have an IRA? Is there a college fund set up for your kids? Do you have an emergency fund? In answer to those questions, I learned that he had a 401(k) with a balance of about $4,500, and that was it. In his mid-forties, he had no savings, no emergency fund, and no other investments.

When we discussed his cash flow he began listing the monthly payments that he made: a mortgage payment, two car payments (one for himself and the other for his wife), a boat payment, and a payment on a four-wheeler. As he continued with the list, I asked if he had considered paying cash for some of those things. The money saved on interest alone would go a long way toward building up his retirement savings. As it was, he had virtually none. His answer floored me: "I can afford the payments."

"Yes, but you have all this stuff. Do you realize how much you have going out each month compared to what you could have going toward retirement?"

A little irritated with me, he replied, "As long as I can afford the payments, I'm in good financial shape."

I tried to point out to him how much his debt load was eating away at his future. The attrition would eventually leave him retired with almost nothing. He looked at me like a deer in headlights, and it became obvious he didn't hear anything I had said.

Many people seem to believe that they will always have some debt. In answer to that, I ask, "Why?" Who says you have to have any debt? The reality is that debt is an enemy, and if you tolerate it, sooner or later, it will chip away at your security and peace of mind, to say nothing of what it will do to your retirement. Don't kid yourself. If you think you are fine just because you can afford the payments, you are not in control of your financial life. Your creditors are. And they won't care whether you are comfortable or not when you retire. They just want their money back.

The time has come in the process of being a Soldier of Finance to recognize debt as your enemy, analyze it, target it, and blow it up. Choose your ammunition and get started. It doesn't matter which method you use. But you need to use one of them.

WARRIOR TASK
Prioritize Debts

Examine your SIT Report and answer the following questions:

1. Which debts are the largest? _____

2. Which debts have the highest interest rates? _____

3. Which debts irritate you the most? _____

With this information fresh in mind, determine which type of debt reduction plan best suits your situation and your temperament:

- **HI Round (High Interest):** Start with the debt that has the highest interest rate.

- **IM Round (Increasing Momentum):** Start with the smallest debt.

- **HE Round (High Emotion):** Start with the most irritating debt.

- **SB Round (Short Burst):** Use any of the first three methods to prioritize your debts, then attack the highest priority in short bursts. Make double payments for two months, followed by a single payment for one month.

Once you prioritize your debts to determine your first target, fill out an Op Order for it.

Op Order

1. Mission Name: _____

2. Define the Mission: _____

3. Time for Completion of the Mission: _____

4. Mission Analysis

   a. Strengths: _____

   b. Weaknesses: _____

5. Plan of Attack: _____

    a. _____

    b. _____

    c. _____

    d. _____

GETTING CASH FLOW POSITIVE

Military actions are not that complicated. Strengths are assessed and then used to defeat the enemy's weaknesses. General Nathan Bedford Forrest is quoted for the simplicity of his approach to warfare: *"Get there first with the most men."* Our training was designed to familiarize us with our resources so that we could defeat any enemy as quickly and as efficiently as possible. Keep it simple and keep it doable.

Defeating debt is not that complicated, either. There are really only two things that have any effect on your financial problems: you can spend less or make more. Any solution is an application of those two concepts. There is nothing else that works.

It really is that simple. Debt strangles your financial security. Eliminating debt results in gaining a handle on your expenses. That means adjusting your cash flow so that you have more coming in than going out. The number one rule of financial stability is to maintain a positive cash flow.

Our problem is that we often ignore the obvious. A woman called one day with some debt issues. I referred her to a friend who is a debt counselor. He chatted with her on the phone, asking questions about her spending habits and jotting down the numbers. After a while, he asked, "You're buying groceries on your credit card, aren't you?"

She was a little taken aback. "How did you know that?" she asked.

"Well," he replied, "you're telling me all your expenses, and how much you make. But I'm not seeing any food on here. I'm pretty sure you're eating, so the only way I can figure that you could do that is to use your credit card."

It should be obvious that buying groceries on credit is not helping to produce a positive cash flow. Keep it simple. How much do you bring home after taxes? How much do you spend? If you spend more than you make, then you need to either cut back on your spending or boost your income.

Go / No Go

Debt Targeting

Have you prioritized the debts listed in your SIT Report?

_____ **Go**   _____ **No Go**

Have you determined which debt reduction plan best suits your situation and your personality?

_____ **Go**   _____ **No Go**

Have you identified lifestyle changes that will help you pay your debt faster?

_____ **Go**   _____ **No Go**

SUMMARY

- Debt is your enemy. The faster you pay it off, the better your life will be.

- Targeting debt should be executed deliberately and methodically.

- The method used to eliminate debt depends on the type of debt and your personality. You can start with the debt that has the highest interest or begin with the smallest debt and work toward the largest. Another option would be to begin with the debt that most irritates you. Whatever method you use, make extra payments to bring down the principal on one debt while making minimum payments on the others. When one is eliminated, focus on the next.

- The Tabata method allows you to make extra payments for two months and then relax a little for one month by making normal payments.

- Never become complacent about debt. Persevere until it is gone.

WEEK 8

SENSITIVE ITEMS REPORT—
TACTICAL BUDGETING

Budgeting sucks. I know there are a few people who enjoy it. My wife actually likes keeping track of our expenses, to the penny. If that describes you, I'm happy for you. You probably don't need this chapter.

But, I think most people agree with me—doing a budget is about as exciting as crawling through a muddy field in the rain. I used to balance my checkbook by checking the available balance printed on my ATM receipt; as long as it showed I had money, regardless of whether or not there were outstanding checks, I felt I was good to go. I know many people who balance their checkbooks each month by looking at the closing balance on their statement and copying it into their check register.

What these methods have in common is that you have no idea where your money goes. Unfortunately, one of the most crucial steps in mastering your finances is getting a grip on your cash flow. Inevitably, this means keeping track of what money comes in and what money goes out. You guessed it—that means the nasty "budget" word.

If you hate budgeting as much as I do, stay with me; we are going to explore ways to overcome your repulsion and make budgeting at least tolerable, if not enjoyable.

You will learn the importance and benefits of budgeting, and, as you begin to see positive results, you will find the process easier. It's not unlike working out: I can't say that I enjoy exercise, either, but I love feeling healthy and having energy for the rest of the day.

TIE BUDGETING TO YOUR GOALS

You don't have to budget all the time. You can take a break from time to time and get away from it; I call it Tactical Budgeting. Your budget becomes part of a specific plan to accomplish a specific mission. Instead of trying to use a detailed budget every day of your life, incorporate it as part of the planning for something that excites you. That shifts the focus from the budget and shines it on your goals.

Similar to the approach to any military campaign, I incorporate a budget into my planning and utilize it partly as a means of setting and accomplishing specific goals and partly to test our financial situation to make sure we can easily handle changes in income.

For example, when we decided to build a house, we had to rearrange our finances. Setting aside money for a down payment and building up a reserve for unexpected expenses, we also planned for furnishings and interior design, along with property taxes and other expenses associated with owning a home. For a time, every penny counted.

Creating a budget to help us accomplish that goal—a line-by-line appraisal of our income and expenses—gave us an accurate picture of our cash flow. It helped us pinpoint unnecessary expenses that could be trimmed, and gave us the vital information we needed to reach our goal.

When the house was finished, we settled back into a routine for our expenditures, and once we knew we had a positive cash flow in our new lifestyle, the budget became superfluous.

Another time we budgeted was when we were preparing for our third son. My wife hated her job and wanted to quit anyway. Due to a company restructure, we knew that when she took maternity leave, it would not be paid, so we decided to use the two-month leave as a test of whether or not we needed that income.

We felt that we were in a financial position to handle the change, but by budgeting and carefully tracking our expenses through that time, we knew with certainty. After our little guy was born, she went back to work for a short time and then quit. The budget not only gave us confidence that we would have no unexpected difficulties, but it helped us make whatever changes were necessary in our spending. Once we settled into the new routine, the budget was no longer necessary.

Don't make a budget your primary mission. Tactical Budgeting is part of planning for a mission. Determine the mission and then create the budget. If your immediate goal is to eliminate debt, then a budget is in order. You need to complete an inventory of your financial life in order to plan effectively. The budget gives you a clear picture of your cash flow situation and what you need to alter in order to take the next step forward in your campaign to overcome debt and achieve wealth.

THE SENSITIVE ITEMS REPORT

As a squad leader, one of my most important responsibilities was to ensure that my squad was ready for action at a moment's notice. Along with my promotion to staff sergeant (E-6) came certain other responsibilities: I had to know where my nine soldiers were at all times, and I had to keep track of any injuries or sickness that might impair their ability to fulfill their duties. In addition, I had to ascertain that all of our equipment worked at all times, and that each man had a minimum of essential gear including weapons, ammunition, water, night vision goggles, and medical supplies. I also had to know where those items were at all times.

We often received orders to be in our Humvees and out the gate in as little as fifteen minutes. In spite of the challenge of keeping everything straight, we never once failed to hit our SP (Starting Point) on time.

The reason we were so successful was the system we had in place to check our equipment on a regular basis—some things weekly, others daily. Called a Sensitive Items Report, it provided a checklist of things to keep up with. The report verified that each man had a weapon, and not just any weapon, but the correct one, right down to the serial number. We checked that we had the correct and required amount of each type of ammunition. We accounted for grenades and flares. Even our Humvees were considered a sensitive item, and we confirmed their serial numbers to be sure we had the right vehicles.

As a regular drill, our drivers carried out a PMCS (Preventive Maintenance Check and Services) to catch potential mechanical problems. We tested radios and checked the .50-caliber machine guns and M249 SAWs (Squad Automatic Weapons). Ammo was examined daily to be certain we had the required amounts and to clean out any sand, which potentially could cause problems.

Repetitive and often redundant, these constant checks were more annoying than I can tell you. They were the military version of budgeting, and they sucked. But the first time we came under fire, I was grateful for those annoying checks; everything worked. The last thing you want to discover in the middle of a firefight is that you didn't bring the ammunition.

THE BASIC TRAINING BUDGET:
IDENTIFY YOUR UNNECESSARY SPENDING

You would be amazed at how little you really need to get by. In the military, I had four uniforms, four sets of PTs, running shoes, socks, boots, toothbrush, razor, notepad, a Bible, and some stamps—the bare essentials. With three meals a day, we were able to make it work. And the truth is, our training prepared us to do with even less if necessary.

The reality for most people is that they spend money on things they don't really need, yet if you ask them, they are sure they can't do without any of it. An important step in getting your finances under control is to understand where your money goes. Your initial budget should be a Basic Training Budget, giving you a clear snapshot of how much you spend unnecessarily.

If you are completely clueless about where your money goes, the place to start is simple record keeping. Gather the facts and analyze your records: your bank statements, receipts, and your credit report. You might also want to keep a record of all your expenditures. Carry a small notebook around with you and write down every penny you spend. You probably will be shocked when you see where your money goes. You can also use a simple spreadsheet with multiple categories to record your spending.

Once you have all the facts, setting up a budget can be as easy as doodling on a napkin. There are budget forms available at office supply stores, or you can choose from a variety of computer programs ranging from Excel spreadsheets to bookkeeping software like QuickBooks. If you're uncomfortable with those, simply use a piece of paper and a pencil. Whichever system you will take the time to use is the one that's best for you.

My wife and I started by breaking down our planned spending into categories. This can be as simple or as complex as you want to make it. A simple budget could have a few categories like "Mortgage," "Utilities," "Food," and "Car." Or you can break it down further with categories such as "Electricity," "Internet," "Cell Phone," and "Water."

Next, collect your most recent pay stubs. If you have a job that regularly pays out a bonus, include that amount. Using this information, project the amount of money that will come in for the next month. Allocate the available money for the categories of expenses. A sample budget might include:

- Rent/Mortgage
- Utilities
- Insurance
- Property Tax
- Contributions

- Phone
- Car Payment(s)
- Satellite/Cable Bill
- Loan Payments

Don't forget to include variable expenses such as:

- Babysitting
- Gifts
- Groceries

- Eating Out
- Fun
- Gas

Include your planned debt reduction efforts in your budget. The purpose of this budget is to accomplish a specific mission, such as paying off a credit card or putting money aside to buy a house. This budget item might be a single entry such as:

- Extra Payment on VISA Card

(For an extensive budget form, with many more categories and specifics, refer to the budgeting form at www.soldieroffinance.com.)

Congratulations! You now have a budget for the next month. The final step is to subtract your projected expenses from your projected income. If the number is less than zero, you have a negative cash flow, and will need to make some adjustments, such as allocating less to eating out, or canceling your cable, or trading in your car for something less expensive. Be creative, but get to a positive cash flow that moves you toward fulfilling your goals. The sooner you achieve the mission objective, the sooner you can stop budgeting for a while.

At first, a budget will feel constrictive, but the truth is you will be liberated by this exercise. Instead of wasting your income on things that don't move you forward, you will redirect your efforts toward your dreams and your goals. With a budget, you can finally gain traction with your money.

ONLINE RESOURCES

A host of online resources are available to help you master budgeting—many of them free. My favorite is www.mint.com. In my opinion, it has become the premier personal finance tool on the web. *Kiplinger's* magazine called it the "Best Budgeting Site," and it was rated a "Top Pick" by *Money* magazine. With www.mint.com you have the ability to upload your account data from your banks, credit unions, credit card companies, lenders, and investments. Having your financial life all in one place helps give you a bird's-eye view of what's going on. Did I mention that it's free?

Look around and find the budgeting tools that work for you. The method you use is not as important as the fact that you are proactively planning a way to get your life under control and making forward progress toward your goals. Whatever type of budget gets the job done is a good budget.

WARRIOR TASK
Plan a Budget

1. Identify a goal that budgeting will help you accomplish and write it down.

2. Set a time for the budget to start and to end.

3. During that period, keep a daily ledger to track all of your expenses so that you can see where your money goes.

4. Revise your budget to reflect areas where you need to cut spending. Follow the revised version for the period of time necessary to accomplish your goal.

DEBRIEFING
Operation Budget

Jim Wang is the creator and editor of the popular personal finance blog "Bargaineering" (www.bargaineering.com). Often quoted in financial publications and on business broadcasts, he still calls himself "a normal guy." When he launched the blog, he knew nothing about handling money, but has since become one of the most respected advisors in the nation. Part of his success is budgeting, as he explains:

(Continues on next page)

"Budgeting is one of the cornerstones of any stable financial life, whether you're a rock star earning six and seven figures or a regular Joe pulling in five. Everyone has a good handle on how much they earn each month, but without a budget, it's difficult to know how much you are spending each month. If you don't know how much you are spending, you won't know how much you're saving and that makes it difficult to plan for the future.

The first step is tracking and recording your spending. I'm a numbers junkie and I started my budget by tracking every penny I spent on anything. Excel was my 'personal finance' software and I tracked everything in it. If you're like me, then open up Excel and start tracking everything. The moment you start doing that, you'll begin playing with the numbers and trying to figure out how to save more and devote more of your hard-earned money to the goals that matter to you!

If you aren't a fan of budgeting or you've failed at it in the past, start with something easier. Start by tracking how much you spend by the dollar, rounding up each time. If you spent $1.50 on a cup of coffee, write down $2. If that is too much for you, consider signing up for a service from a site like Mint that will look through your credit card transactions, categorize them, and produce lovely reports that explain where you are spending your salary.

The next step is to improve your budget by finding areas of your spending you can trim. If you find yourself spending too much in one area, make a concerted effort to pare back those expenses. When I first started budgeting, I noticed I was spending too much money eating at 'restaurants,' which included the cafeteria at work. Every day I'd spend at least $7 or $8 on lunch, which was a $40 weekly drain on my budget. In the span of 52 weeks, that's a solid $2,080 each year on lunch alone. I really enjoyed eating lunch with my friends in the cafeteria, but I could eat better food by bringing in leftovers or preparing my own lunch.

Eventually, you'll get into a monthly rhythm where your expenses won't change too much because you've fallen into a pattern. Remember to occasionally revisit your budget to see if you are still on track,

spending about the same in each category, and whether your priorities
have changed.

   If you've never budgeted before, I highly recommend giving it a try.
Stick with it for at least two months. If you still hate doing it and can't
stand to do it, then at least you now understand where you've been
spending your money the last two months. You'll find that budgeting is
one of the easiest, cheapest, and more valuable ways to get a better
sense of your current financial situation and the direction you're going."

PRACTICE MAKES PERFECT: WHY SOLDIERS DRILL

My memory of the early days in training can be summed up in one
word: chaos. We completed drills over and over again to teach us how
to deal with a variety of situations that could occur on the battlefield.
Our primary mode of transportation was typically a convoy of three
Humvees. If the lead truck went down, the response would be different from what it would be if the middle or rear vehicle was hit.

   Driving through the woods one day, simulating a standard patrol,
one of the instructors suddenly jumped out from cover, popped
smoke to simulate an explosion, and barked out the scenario: "This
Humvee's hit, gunner's down, driver's down. Go!"

   The first time, no one was sure who should grab the radio, so
everyone talked into their radios and communication got lost in the
chatter of voices. The instructor then further complicated the drill;
he told us we were taking sniper fire, and didn't know where it was
coming from. We weren't sure who was supposed to secure the injured or who should call for a medivac. Two trucks were called when
only one was needed, adding to the general confusion.

   Then came the task of attempting to carry a 200-pound
wounded soldier—with his heavy gear—from one truck to another.
Just getting him out of the tight fit inside the Humvee was a comical
and pathetic sight.

Had we really been in combat, we all would have died. We had no idea what we were doing and had never worked together as a team. Nor had we learned our assignments properly . . . yet.

Two months later, after practicing that drill over and over and over and over, it was a different story. Battle drills taught us how to work with each other, what to expect, how to depend on our Battle Buddies, and how to get the job done without panic or confusion. The first time we came under fire in Iraq, I was glad we had practiced those drills. Reacting with cool confidence was far less a matter of courage than it was training and practice.

FAMILY BATTLE DRILLS

Budgeting is a family project. Everyone needs to be on the same page. If you cut expenses but your spouse does not, you'll be fighting each other and not gaining much ground. As every frontline soldier knows, you're only as strong as the support team behind you.

You must sit down with your entire family and together devise a plan of action that you can all stick to. Honest communication is essential for this mission. There may be things that you will have to give up in order to get your debt under control: hobbies, shopping sprees, golf outings, pedicures, gadgets, etc.

I want to inject a comment here about separate checking accounts, where the husband has *his* money and the wife has *her* money. I have come across this arrangement quite a few times, and it not only puzzles me, it concerns me, especially when a family is struggling to overcome debt. When you agreed to join together in marriage, "Till death do us part," you agreed to be together. Keeping your money separate implies that you have separate goals and different directions that are important to you.

Lack of unity in planning often creates difficulties in gaining control of finances. Separate accounts may seem trivial, but they usually accompany a limited amount of communication or agreement about financial goals. Both are necessary in order to achieve success.

Working together to defeat your financial enemies involves preparation for every possibility. Once you get your budget in order and you see your situation clearly, it is beneficial to walk through different scenarios to see what would happen if there were extreme changes to your expenses or your income. Run your own Battle Drills and visualize what would happen if suddenly you were laid off from your job. What would happen if you needed to replace your furnace? Could you make it if the price of gasoline doubled? Battle Drills help you prepare for these situations and point out any areas you haven't thought about.

To get the most out of your Battle Drills, use the following Battle Drill Checklist as a basis for your family meeting. Discuss these questions and any others that arise in relation to your financial future. The key to successful Battle Drills is communication. This doesn't need to take a long time, but everyone in the family needs to be familiar with the financial situation and with your plans and goals. You need to function as a team to make this work.

Go / No Go
Battle Drill
Are you clear on your objective?
_____ **Go**   _____ **No Go**
Is your objective written down and posted?
_____ **Go**   _____ **No Go**

(Continues on next page)

Are you current on your bills and your creditors?

_____ **Go** _____ **No Go**

Are you properly insured? Where are the insurance policies stored? Does everyone know where to find them in case of an emergency?

_____ **Go** _____ **No Go**

Do you have some liquid cash savings? Where are they, and who has access to them?

_____ **Go** _____ **No Go**

Is everyone in the family familiar with the budget? Do they know what each family member is allowed to spend in each category, particularly recreational expenses?

_____ **Go** _____ **No Go**

Who is responsible for paying specific bills? Who keeps the checkbook up-to-date?

_____ **Go** _____ **No Go**

How does each family member report expenses in order to keep track of them?

_____ **Go** _____ **No Go**

Are there resources available for assisting with any of your record keeping that you have not explored?

_____ **Go** _____ **No Go**

How are responsibilities delegated?

_____ **Go** _____ **No Go**

What actions will you take if the primary income earner in the family is laid off or unable to work?

_____ **Go**   _____ **No Go**

SUMMARY

■ Tactical Budgeting allows you the freedom to not be tied to a budget when you don't need to be. This method helps you to make use of budgets for limited periods of time to accomplish specific goals, such as buying a house or planning a vacation.

■ A budget is used to determine exactly where your money goes and identify things that you don't need to spend money on. By keeping track of spending for a period of time, you will see how much you spend unnecessarily.

■ Setting up a Basic Training Budget begins with analyzing your records, receipts, bank statements, and credit reports. Take note of where your money goes.

■ Use this information to create a budget by categorizing expenses—rent/mortgage, phone, utilities, car payment, and other expenses. Fill in the expenses for each category so that you can set limits on your spending and keep track of it.

■ Online resources are available to assist with budgeting. Find one that works best for you.

■ Train yourself and your family to follow budget guidelines by having Family Battle Drills. Involve the entire family in discussions of how you will plan your spending.

WEEK 9

FRAGO—THE SAVINGS ACCOUNTS SURVIVAL GUIDE

As long as we were in a combat area, we were always ready. One thing we rarely did was take off our boots. In case of an emergency, it took too long to lace them back up. Many times I ran down the hallway, pulling on my vest, balancing my helmet on my head while hoping I didn't drop my M-16. All those things can be done while running, but you have to have your boots on.

Emergencies don't wait until you're ready. If you aren't prepared and ready to take them in stride, they will cause you problems. You can't anticipate everything, but you can prepare for the unexpected. Once you have your budget laid out, you know which things are

expected. Now it's time to think about setting aside funds for events you can't predict.

Most Americans do not have any contingency plan set up if the unexpected occurs. They assume that as long as they are working, everything's fine. If an emergency comes up, they pull out their credit cards, which adds to their debt and further undermines their financial future.

The economic collapse of 2008 took many by surprise. People who thought they could coast to retirement were suddenly looking for work, and jobs were hard to find. They quickly discovered that unemployment benefits were not nearly as much as their income had been, and they last for only a certain amount of time.

Job loss is not the only emergency you may face. You also never know when your family will be hit with unplanned medical bills. Insurance helps, and we'll talk about that in Chapter 16. Even with insurance, however, there is likely to be a lapse between the moment you need the help and the moment it arrives. While you're waiting, you don't want to spend time worrying about basic things, such as how to put food on the table.

THE FRAGO FUND

"No plan ever survives contact with the enemy." This is a paraphrase of a statement by Prussian Field Marshal Helmuth von Moltke. If you want to be completely accurate, the original quote was: *"No plan of operations extends with any certainty beyond the first contact with the main hostile force."* I find the shorter version easier to remember.

What von Moltke meant was very simple; there are always things you cannot predict. You must have the means of adjusting your plans on the basis of new contingencies. The Army has a name for these midcourse corrections; they call it FRAGO, which stands for "Fragmentary Order." A FRAGO provides changes to an existing order.

As a Soldier of Finance, you will occasionally make adjustments based on emergencies or unexpected events. Your FRAGO will have a different meaning; I call it a Financial Reserve and Goal Fund (FRAGO Fund). Essentially, this is an emergency fund, but it's a little more than that. You now have specific objectives in your life that you are working to complete and you're no longer living your life aimlessly from paycheck to paycheck. You're moving forward and want to minimize interruptions in pursuing your goals. By developing an emergency reserve, you avoid taking too long of a hiatus in your cash flow. You have enough cash on hand to keep you going for a period of time. This allows you to deal with any minor emergencies, like a car breakdown or repairs on your house.

The goal for an emergency fund is to put aside enough money to keep your bills paid and enable you to live for a period of time if your income were to suddenly stop. Ideally, you should have enough money to live for three months. That gives you time to make whatever adjustments are necessary. If you were laid off, it allows time to look for other work or to set up unemployment benefits. If you face a medical crisis, this gives you time for insurance to kick in.

While three months is ideal, you need at least one month of living expenses on hand. How much money should you have in your FRAGO Fund? Many financial advisors recommend a simple amount like $1,000. That's not a bad place to start, but you need to consider your geographic location. If you live in the Midwest, $1,000 is a workable reserve. If you live in Los Angeles, $1,000 won't last much more than a week. A simple formula can be used to determine how much should be in your emergency fund:

BAH (Basic Allowance for Housing)
+ ME (Monthly Expenses)
= FRAGO Fund minimum

BAH is a military term for Basic Allowance for Housing. This represents your mortgage payment or your rent.

ME represents your monthly expenses. This includes utilities, food, and the minimum payment on your loans and credit cards. These numbers should be easily accessed from your current budget.

FRAGO Fund calculation is the minimum required amount. Of course, if you can build up the fund, do so. But don't lose sight of your primary missions, which is wiping out your debt.

WARRIOR TASK
Create a FRAGO Fund

1. Using your basic budget from Chapter 10, determine how much money you need for one month.

2. Open a savings account, if you don't already have one.

3. Decide on an amount that you will deposit into your savings account from each paycheck until you have a minimum amount accumulated.

WATCH OUT FOR IMPOSTERS

In combat, we always wore camouflage. Our uniforms were designed to match the terrain. Vehicles were painted in colors that would blend in with the ground. Netting was pulled over gun emplacements and bunkers to make them as difficult to see as possible. The object is to deceive the enemy regarding your location, strength, and abilities.

Of course, the enemy is always doing the same thing; they don't want you to know their weaknesses. Unfortunately, when it comes to dealing with emergencies, many people think they have cash because they have credit. They are not the same thing. Don't be fooled by imposters that try to make you think you have cash on hand. Here are the major imposters to watch out for:

Imposter #1: Credit Cards. Having access to a cash advance on your credit card does not mean you have cash. Stop fooling yourself. When you have to pay 20% interest for any cash you borrow, you're just digging yourself deeper into a financial hole.

Imposter #2: HELOCs (Home Equity Lines of Credit). Equity in your home is as good as cash, right? Wrong! When you take out a line of credit on your home, you're just digging yourself a deeper hole and potentially putting yourself at financial risk. Here's why:

1. HELOCs are debt. You're borrowing money, which further compounds the problem. When you're borrowing money to make a payment and eventually have to start making payments on the amount you borrowed, there's something terribly wrong.

2. They may disappear. Since the financial crisis of 2008, the rules and availability of HELOCs have changed. If you're banking on being able to borrow and that is your only option, you might be in for a rude awakening. You'll have no cash and no HELOC.

3. You put your home at risk. While serving overseas, it was imperative to have constant security on our base to keep potential threats out. Taking out a HELOC is as potentially dangerous as it would have been to allow anyone on our base before inspecting him or her. With a HELOC, you use your home as collateral. What happens when you can't make the payment on your HELOC because you lose your job? You'll get a true taste of what it really means to "sleep in the field." You will lose your home. It's not worth the risk until you have a sufficient savings account.

Imposter #3: Payday Loans. Take out one of these and you'll have easy access to cash with an equally impressive interest rate, somewhere between 200% and 500%. I witnessed one that carried a mind-numbing 521%! Payday loans carry all the problems of a credit card multiplied many times over. Many people who get sucked into these loans fall into a vicious cycle that's harder to break than a nicotine habit.

Imposter #4: Your Stuff. Have you ever thought that if things get really bad, you can just head to the pawnshop and hock your goods? Don't bank on it. Right now pawnshops are overrun with people thinking the same thing, and they are leaving disappointed. If you think you have liquidity because you own an iPod, you will be shocked when you learn what it's worth. You'll be lucky to get 25 percent at best. Do you think your gold-plated pendant will help pay the next light bill? Good luck. It's likely you won't get a dime for it.

MAKING THE MOST OF YOUR SAVINGS ACCOUNT

I mentioned earlier how eventful my first patrol in Baghdad was. To prepare for that day, it was important that I knew the terrain and what to expect. To get a feel for the area, I went over the route with a veteran team the day before. In combat, you can never be too prepared. Knowing that lives could be lost if we weren't ready was incentive enough.

The particular road was one of the hottest in Iraq; a major incident had occurred there every day for the past two months. To say my adrenaline was high would be an understatement, but I was with guys who had been there.

I was also with guys who had become complacent. I sat in the back of a Humvee, observing landmarks along the route and taking mental notes. In front of me, the squad leader's head slumped back and his eyes closed. A minute later, his mouth was open and he started snoring.

This must be a well-trained team, I thought, if the leader trusts them so much he can take a nap in one of the most dangerous areas in the country. I wasn't sure whether to be impressed or afraid. The question was answered soon, when I noticed that the gunner in the turret was snoozing, too. I guess he figured that if it was okay for the staff sergeant, it must be okay for him. Except, this was the guy who was supposed to be on alert for potential problems along the patrol route. That was the whole point of this exercise. Thank God the driver stayed awake—he was the only one. And thank God nothing happened that day.

That experience left me bewildered. How could anyone be that nonchalant when so much was at stake? I couldn't understand it. When it comes to financial security, I see the same thing repeatedly. The establishment of emergency funds is one of those areas in which complacency proves to be commonplace.

I suppose it's the fact that most of the time nothing happens, and, after a while, people assume nothing *will* happen. They tell themselves, "Yes, I need a reserve fund in case something happens, but I'll get that done tomorrow. There's plenty of time." Then the transmission goes and there's no means to fix it without using a credit card. Or the boss hands out pink slips at work. And there is nothing to live on.

To be successful, you must be vigilant. Not even an act as simple as putting money into a savings account should be taken for granted. Shop around and explore your possibilities. Don't assume you're getting the highest interest rate at your local institution.

It's true that savings accounts pay next to nothing anyway. They are not the kind of investment that will make you rich. Keep in mind that the primary purpose of keeping your FRAGO Fund in savings is so you can access it quickly if you need it. That doesn't mean, however, that you should not take the trouble to get the most out of it. Here are a few considerations when building up a savings account:

- **Make sure you have enough in your savings account.** If there isn't enough to cover your emergency expenses, it won't be a very useful fund in the event of an emergency. Be aware that many banks charge a fee if your average balance falls below a certain point. Learn what that amount is and keep your account balance above it.

- **Make sure you get the best interest rate possible.** Nothing says you have to put your money in the bank on the corner. Shop around. Check other banks and institutions, including online institutions, and find the best return for your money. You might as well make something on it. (For more ideas about where you can get the highest interest rates around, please refer to www.soldieroffinance.com/resources.)

- **Make sure you don't have too much in your savings account.** The first consideration, of course, is to make sure you have enough to live on for at least a month. A little more than the minimum is good, but if you put too much in the account, you will have your money sitting around without giving you a good return on investment. This was a problem I faced early in my career. My wife and I understood the importance of a reserve for emergencies, so we tucked away a sizable amount of money. But we realized later that we could have gotten much better interest rates if we had shopped around a little more.

Some people have what I would consider an exorbitant amount in savings. There are other investment options paying a much higher return. We'll explore some of these options in the upcoming chapters. You really don't need much more than three months' expenses in your emergency fund. That allows plenty of time to liquidate other investments if necessary.

Be prepared for emergencies, but once that is covered, project into the future and establish a plan for building wealth. Your lifetime campaign is not about mere survival; it's about winning in the end. Stay on top of all your investments and be sure they're producing, including your savings account.

YOU ARE NOW READY FOR ANYTHING

Hopefully by now you are feeling more confident. By faithfully following the Soldier of Finance procedures, you have positioned yourself for the final phase of your campaign to take control of your financial life. Take a moment to reflect on the progress you've made.

Most important, you've gotten the upper hand over the strongest opponents to your success. You've identified your weaknesses and your strengths. You've put your credit cards in their place and have gotten your debt under control. By establishing clearly defined goals, you've provided for emergencies and given yourself the means to adjust your plans when necessary.

These are not small accomplishments. You are now in a secure place to begin making investments that can move you into wealth. Too many people try to invest without securing their foundation. Their bad financial habits and accumulated debt undermine their future. But you have not gone that route. You took the time to get ready for the fun part of being a Soldier of Finance: conquering prosperity. Congratulations.

Go / No Go

Preparation for Emergencies

Do you have a FRAGO Fund?

_____ **Go**   _____ **No Go**

How much money is in your FRAGO Fund? How long could you last if your income completely stopped?

_____ **Go**   _____ **No Go**

Where is your FRAGO Fund?

_____ **Go**   _____ **No Go**

How much interest are you getting on the money when you are not using it?

_____ **Go**   _____ **No Go**

How long would it take you to access your FRAGO Fund if you needed it?

_____ **Go**   _____ **No Go**

SUMMARY

- You cannot predict emergencies, but you can prepare for the impact they will have on your financial situation. Preparation allows you to be flexible enough to meet whatever situation comes along.

- Create a FRAGO Fund (Financial Reserve and Goal Fund), and set aside enough money to use during unexpected emergencies, such as loss of a job or a car breakdown.

- Your FRAGO Fund should have, as a minimum, the amount of money you would need to cover your expenses for a month. Three months is better, and you should work toward that goal.

- A simple formula for knowing how much to put in your FRAGO Fund is to add your basic allowance for housing (BAH) to your monthly expenses (ME). The resulting number is the minimum you should have on hand.

- Do not use any form of credit as an emergency fund, such as credit cards, HELOCs (Home Equity Lines of Credit), or payday loans. Adding to your debt will only make matters worse. Your goal is to get out of debt.

- A FRAGO Fund should be kept in a savings account so that it is readily accessible on short notice. By leaving it there, you will collect at least a small amount of interest while the money is waiting.

- Don't put too much in a savings account. You will be losing money on interest.

WEEK 10

MANUALS AND ORDERS— GETTING STARTED IN INVESTING

One constant in the military was that we were provided with as much information as could be accumulated. In Basic Training, we had the *Soldier's Handbook*. In Iraq, every time we launched an operation, it began with comprehensive Operation Orders spelling out the mission and our objective, covering every conceivable scenario. No matter what happened, no matter what might go wrong, we would be prepared to react quickly and decisively. The platoon sergeant was responsible for passing information down to us. As a squad leader, my job was to make sure my team leaders understood everything they needed to know for the mission. We ran battle drills until it all worked like a well-oiled machine. Ignorance was no excuse.

Yet ignorance is one of the biggest reasons people don't start investing. They either don't know how to start or they harbor misconceptions about how investments work that lead them to believe it's not worth the effort.

Several years ago, I met with a guy who needed some help with his pension. The plant where he worked had shut down and the employees had to make decisions about their pensions and their 401(k) plans. He had a pension because participation was required. When I asked about his 401(k), however, I discovered that he had turned it down ten years earlier.

"I didn't want to mess with that," he told me, "because it involved the stock market."

Based on that one factor, he decided not to take advantage of a great opportunity to put some money aside for his retirement. His employer had a great matching plan. And the sad part is that a 401(k) does not require you to invest in stocks. You can choose bonds or money market options. A 401(k) is not the stock market. His ignorance left him near retirement with very little saved or invested.

WHY HAVEN'T YOU STARTED?

I recently e-mailed my newsletter group and asked the question, "Why haven't you started investing yet?" It was a loaded question, of course, because the majority of my readers are 40 or older and already are investing, but I do have many younger subscribers and I was curious to know what holds people back.

Responses varied, but I noticed that most fell into two basic areas: some didn't have the patience to wait out an investment; others didn't think they had enough money to get started. One guy told me, "I feel like I need $100,000 to get started."

You will need patience. There is no way to get around that. Investments that provide security and wealth will not fill your bank account in a month. They take time. At the start of my career, I met with an older couple who were in their mid-seventies. They had purchased a bond through my office, a transaction done over the phone, and I wanted to meet them face-to-face and work with their investments. I drove forty-five minutes to the next town to sit down with them in their home.

As they filled in some background information for me, I discovered that they didn't really know how wealthy they were. The husband had spent his whole life as a line worker at a car factory. His wife was a retired teacher.

They had not done anything spectacular. In the beginning, every time they got a paycheck, they bought some savings bonds. As time went on, they branched out into a few stocks, bonds, and mutual funds. Now they lived comfortably off their pensions and never pulled money from their investments. Totaling their assets, we discovered they had accumulated over $1 million.

In the case of this couple, they had almost too much patience. They put money away steadily and paid no attention to it. They retired and didn't even know how rich they were!

Investments pay off over time. The nature of this multiplication process is that for a long time it doesn't seem like you're making much progress. You feel like you're running on a treadmill, but at some point, the numbers increase rapidly and dramatically. (See Figure 12-1 for an example.)

If you don't start, however, you will never see that kind of return. If you don't have the patience to let it grow, you will never get started.

I began investing with $50 a month. I had a job with an investment firm, making $18,500 base salary. That was not back in the 1970s, either, when you could live on that; it was in 2002! My budget was tight. After deductions, my take-home pay was less than $850 each month.

Figure 12-1 ■ Example of retirement savings growth.

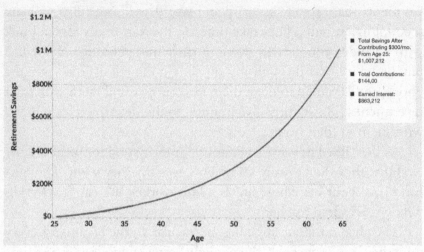

Nevertheless, I understood the value of getting started early. I opened a Roth IRA and set aside $50 every month to invest. At the same time, I opened a 401(k) and put 5 percent of my income before tax into it. In two years, that $50 initial monthly investment grew to $1,200 plus accumulated interest. That might not seem like much, but by the time I retire, it will be in the millions.

ARE YOU READY?

Eliminate the excuses that have kept you from investing. You don't need much to get started, and it's not difficult to learn the basics. Understand the importance of taking action. I've never met anybody who decided, after looking at their financial profile, that they had saved too much.

Like any good military operation, you have to make a plan, think it through, and execute it patiently and consistently. Many people have the idea that they will acquire enough for retirement by winning the lottery. The truth is, they have a better chance of going on a date with Kim Kardashian or Justin Bieber. Building wealth for your future is not a dramatic spin of the roulette wheel, but a methodical process that takes time.

THE MAGIC 10 PERCENT:
A GUIDELINE FOR INVESTING

Ten percent is a number that appears throughout history as a standard for a variety of financial applications. Church people are familiar with tithing, the practice of giving 10 percent of their income to support their ministry.

A pastor I know speculates that 10 percent is often used because we have ten fingers, which makes it simple for anyone to calculate, including those who don't understand math. It is a convenient number to work with, and it provides a simple way to calculate how you can allocate money for investments.

As a first step in the investment process, consider what you can do with 10 percent of your income. Develop the habit of disciplining yourself, setting aside a portion of each paycheck for something other than bills and living expenses. Starting with 10 percent is a simple way to do that.

You should always pay yourself first, before you pay your creditors. And by that, I don't mean taking 10 percent and going to the mall. I mean putting 10 percent into your future. Twenty percent would be better, but if you're just getting started, 10 percent will be less intimidating. Once you get into the habit of paying yourself, you will be able to expand the amount you put into investments, but for now, reference 10 percent as a bare minimum.

Before describing the types of investment vehicles available to you, however, I want to address a subject that I believe is an important aspect of financial stability—giving. I have made it a practice to always give 10 percent of my income to my church. If you are not religious, develop the habit of making charitable contributions to a cause close to your heart.

There are many benefits to giving. First is the basic concept that you get what you give. This idea has been expressed in numerous ways; "You reap what you sow" and "What goes around comes around" are two common ones. I don't know that I can really explain it, but good things come to generous people. When you develop an overall attitude of generosity, other aspects of how you interact with people are affected. You become friendlier, meaning people are more likely to want to be around you, more likely to be generous toward you, and more likely to share opportunities with you that they otherwise wouldn't.

It's no accident that people who are successful in business are also good at building strong personal relationships with people. They establish trust through their approachability and integrity. Trust leads to more business opportunities and greater success. By this obscure route, generosity is a link to financial success.

The key is that you have to mean it. People can tell when you just put on a friendly face to make a sale. Generosity, when you don't get anything back, indicates a lot about you and is a character trait well worth developing. Where you give is not as important as the fact that you do. If your motive is getting a tax deduction, you have missed the point entirely, and the charitable contribution will probably not help you much.

Consider setting aside 10 percent of your paycheck to give away; mathematically, it might not make much sense to you, but the benefits reach far beyond the dollars and cents involved.

Next, set aside another 10 percent for investments. A Brightwork Partners survey of 3,300 working Americans found that workers who were best prepared for retirement—that is, those on track to replace 100 percent of their current income—differed from those likely to replace 45 percent or less of their current income, not in how much they earned but in how much they utilized savings plans. The former saved 10 percent of their income and invested it where it would gain interest.

The point is that you don't need much to start investing, and if you don't know where to begin, look right under your nose. You get a paycheck. Before you do anything with it, before you pay a single bill, before you go out to dinner or go to a movie, take one-tenth of it and put it somewhere that will let it work for you.

GET THE RIGHT ADVICE

Another aspect of investing is getting good advice. Friends and family will try to tell you the best way to invest, based on their own experience, but ultimately, they probably only know what they've been involved in. Take the time to learn as much as you can about how money works, and trust your own judgment. That does not mean you should not consult financial professionals. Full-time advisors spend a lot of time keeping up with current investment vehicles, trends, and changing tax laws. The more complex your investments become, the more advice you probably will need.

How do you choose a good advisor? How do you know if the advisor is trustworthy? Here are three considerations:

1. **Don't sign with the first person you talk to.** Take the time to interview at least two or three advisors. Listen to what they offer. Chat with each one long enough to be sure you are comfortable with the advisor's background, education, and personality. If you ask a question and do not get a direct answer, or what you hear doesn't make sense to you, that person may not be a good fit.

2. **Ask how the advisor gets paid.** Many advisors are paid by commission, which translates to a predisposition to recommend investment vehicles that yield the best commissions for them. That will likely be the best investment for the advisor, but not necessarily for you. Look for fee-based or fee-only

advisors. They are paid with a percentage of your account, which means the more money you make, the more they make, providing the incentive to find the best investments they can for you. That doesn't mean you should never talk to someone who takes commissions, but be sure you understand the advisor's methods and motivation.

3. **See if there are any complaints filed against the advisor.** There are a couple of places you can check to see if an advisor has negative reviews from past clients. One is www.CFP.net, the Certified Financial Planner Board of Standards. Do a local search to check on certified financial planners in your area. Another site that deals with fee-only advisors is www.NAPFA.org, the National Association of Personal Financial Advisors.

SECURE YOUR BASE OF OPERATIONS

Each operation I was involved in in Iraq started from our base. We often drove patrols into hostile territory, where we were on our guard for roadside bombs, snipers, or any other kind of attack. No matter what happened on patrol, we always had a degree of security. Nothing was ever planned without provision for links with the base of operations—our source of information about other units, fuel and ammunition, and anything else we needed. A good base was always established, fortified, and made secure before we branched out into the surrounding areas.

Similarly, be sure you have a solid base before you begin investing. Keep your priorities straight and use common sense. There is a reason we dealt with debt and credit cards first. If you haven't taken care of those issues, you are not ready to invest. It's pointless to invest money in a mutual fund, hoping to make 10%, when you're paying

20% interest on a credit card. If you haven't eliminated those interest payments, that should be your priority, not rushing out to jump into the stock market. You'll make more money paying off the debt first.

Make sure your FRAGO Fund is secure and that you've paid down your debt. Only then will you be ready to consider investments.

Go / No Go

Preparation for Investing

Have you identified the reasons you have not invested in the past?

_____ **Go**   _____ **No Go**

How much money do you think you need to get started?

_____ **Go**   _____ **No Go**

(Continues on next page)

Do you give regularly to any charities?

_____ **Go**   _____ **No Go**

Have you considered working with a financial advisor?

_____ **Go**   _____ **No Go**

Are your debts paid off?

_____ **Go**   _____ **No Go**

Is your FRAGO Fund in place?

_____ **Go**   _____ **No Go**

SUMMARY

- The reason people don't invest primarily falls into a couple of categories: They don't know how to start, or they don't believe they have enough available money to start. Additionally, they often lack the patience to allow investments to grow to maturity.

- You don't need much to begin. Start with a small amount deposited into a savings account until it builds up to a sufficient amount for other investments.

- Ten percent is a good point of reference, resulting in the minimum amount you should pay to yourself before you do anything else. Twenty percent is better, but put at least 10 percent into your future.

■   Develop a habit of giving. Whether to your church or another charitable organization, giving brings benefits in everything you do.   An attitude of generosity aids in creating
stronger relationships with your community, neighbors, business associates, and clients.

■   When looking for a financial advisor, take the time to interview more than one. Ask lots of questions and, above all, ask
how they are paid in order to determine whether or not
commissions they might receive will influence their advice.
Fee-based and fee-only advisors are usually best.

■   You can check with www.NAPFA.org and www.CFP.net to
see if an advisor has negative reviews from past clients.

■   Pay off debts before investing. It is foolish to pay 20% interest
on a credit card while you put money into an investment
that only brings in 10% profit.

■   Make sure your FRAGO Fund is established before you attempt any other investments.

WEEK 11

FROM BOOTS TO HUMVEES—BEGINNING INVESTMENT VEHICLES

I covered a lot of ground over the duration of my military career. Even when stationed in one place, it seemed we were constantly on the move, and a variety of vehicles were required to transport us. The appropriate means of transportation largely depended on the purpose of our movement.

In Basic Training, I quickly learned that our main source of transportation was our boots. Our boots transported us nearly everywhere we needed to go, rain or shine. Our drill sergeant constantly reminded us to take good care of our feet, which were more important than our M-16s. If we didn't take care of them, we were as good as dead.

From the beginning, we learned how important our feet were. We marched to chow. We marched to the PX. We marched to get our hair cut. We marched to almost every single M-16 range. We marched to a parade field just so we could practice marching! During this stretch of training, I learned the true meaning of the expression "My dogs are barking," because my feet never stopped barking at me.

The advantage of boots is glaringly obvious when you have to move under fire or travel into areas where a vehicle provides too big a target. Boots are slow, but in many circumstances, they are very practical in terms of accomplishing your mission. The limitation of boots is the inability to carry you over long distances quickly.

When I transferred units and became a field artilleryman, my mode of transportation changed. Since we were always hauling out the "big gun"—the howitzer—we rode in the back of a six-wheeled, five-ton truck. The bed of the truck was lined with wooden benches.

Our missions in Iraq were normally run with up-armored Humvees. Although they looked big and spacious, we always joked that they were designed for guys no taller than 5'5". You could never ride in them without banging a knee or an elbow against something. In spite of that drawback, a Humvee provided an optimum balance

of protection against snipers and roadside bombs, while allowing plenty of mobility and maneuverability in confined city streets.

For my buddies who served in Afghanistan's mountainous terrain, the preferred vehicle was a 14-ton MRAP (Mine Resistant Ambush Protected) vehicle. These heavy mama-jamas were utilized because of their resistance to roadside bombs. Boasting more armor than any other military vehicle created, its V-shaped hull enabled it to deflect bombs that detonated underneath it.

Of all the military transportation I experienced, the most memorable was the two times I rode in a C-130 transport aircraft. Each trip was accompanied by powerful emotions. Flying into Iraq, we landed and taxied to a stop. The back door dropped and we stepped out into the Baghdad sunlight, signifying the commencement of my deployment. I didn't know what to expect. I remember thinking, "Do I need to have a gun?" "Should I look for a Humvee?" The exhilaration of being somewhere exotic and new soon wore off as I settled into the routine, but I still recall the intensity of those first moments.

The second time was the trip out. Lugging rucksacks behind us, we boarded the C-130. I sat in one of the seats along the outer shell of the plane, packed in tightly with my gear between two other soldiers, unable to move and sweltering in the desert heat. Finally the plane lumbered down the runway and into the air. The airflow started to cool things off and it got a little more comfortable. But there's no such thing as a smooth ride on a C-130, and it wasn't long before I got airsick.

In spite of the discomforts, I knew my deployment was over and I was finally going home. I didn't care how I got there; as long as we were moving, nothing else mattered. To this day, that memory gives me goose bumps.

REMEMBER THE MISSION

In the military the terrain and the objective determine the mode of transportation utilized. Similarly, when it comes to saving or investing for retirement, you need to choose the right investment vehicle to accomplish your goal.

In my business, I often meet clients who have no plan of attack when it comes to investments. Instead, they utilize whatever comes along first, which is often not the best way to get them to where they need to be. People with short-term goals invest money into vehicles better designed for retirement accounts. The problem is, they lose sight of the mission objectives. The end result determines the plan. When you forget the mission, you are destined for failure.

USE BOOTS, NOT BUSES, FOR SHORT DISTANCES

When it came to traveling shorter distances, the only appropriate mode of transportation was walking. It never made sense to take the time to load forty troops on a bus and complete a head count to make sure everyone was on board only to dismount two blocks later.

When it comes to short-term savings, it doesn't make sense to use long-term investments. You want to keep them as liquid as possible. And by liquid, I don't mean wet like a Navy SEAL. Liquid means that you can access the money quickly.

Like a soldier, you have to be ready on the fly. Throughout my military career we constantly ran battle drills to see how quickly we could get ready. When it comes to dealing with financial emergencies, you don't want to have to wait an extended period of time to get your money.

I once had a conversation with a recent college graduate who wanted to invest some of his graduation money in stocks. He had heard from his family and friends that it was a good time to get in because the market was down. I couldn't argue with that logic, but as we talked further, it became clear that his goal was not long term. He planned to live off the investment while he attended graduate school.

The problem was a short-term goal in a long-term investment. If you expect to need the money in less than three years, never, never, never, never invest in the stock market. There is far too much fluctuation. Think of the stock market as a roller coaster. You start out pretty comfortable, fasten your seat belt, sit back, and take a deep breath of anticipation. You start to move forward, slowly climbing to the top of the first rise. Then everything changes. Suddenly you're plummeting, and your stomach rises into your throat. Just when you think you've adjusted to that, you take a sudden turn that throws you into the side of the car. You loop around several times and plummet again at a breathtaking rate. You finally slow down and start climbing again. But at the top, the whole giddy ride starts over.

The ups and downs of a roller coaster are great fun when you know that within a couple of minutes you will be back where you started and you can climb out onto solid ground again—unless you had a chili dog right before the ride! Roller coasters are ridden for the thrill.

You do not want that kind of thrill when you're trying to pay your monthly expenses. You want to know you have money there.

Ask anyone who invested in stocks in 2008 how stable and secure they felt the first week in October of that year. Those who could afford to wait out the market will eventually get to the top again, but if you depend on being able to liquidate your investment quickly, you run a tremendous risk. Trying to invest in the market and make a little return in the short term is never worth seeing your savings cut in half.

To illustrate, let's compare a money market account with stocks. Let's say you have $10,000 to put into your savings and you're considering investing in the stock market. Your bank is offering 2% on its money market accounts, but your coworkers keep bragging about how they've made 15% in the past couple of months and call you a schmuck for not jumping on this gold mine. Rather than an emotional knee-jerk reaction, take the time to actually run the numbers:

> **Bank:** $10,000 × 2% Interest = $10,200
> **Stock Market:** $10,000 × 15% Potential Return = $11,500

You took a considerably greater risk and netted $1,300 more. Of course, this is one of those "best case" scenarios equivalent to never hitting a red light or traffic on your way to work. Yes, it can happen, but how often? What if the stock market dropped instead of going up, and you needed the money now?

> **Bank:** $10,000 × 2% Interest = $10,200
> **Stock Market:** $10,000 × 20% Loss = $8,000

That's a net loss of $2,200—not a good short investment. Two typical reactions to such loss will make it worse: (1) you leave it invested and wait for it to break even, or (2) you invest it even more aggressively, trying to make back what you lost. If there was ever an act that epitomized the expression "shooting yourself in the foot," this is it. Don't do it. The pain isn't worth it. Save the roller coaster experience for amusement parks.

One of the biggest mistakes I see many people make is the attempt to make a quick buck. It rarely turns out well. The stock market is for investments that you can leave for a long time—which brings us to the right vehicle for the short term. Savings accounts are tough for a lot of people to swallow. They're boring. They don't pay anything. You don't hear Jim Cramer screaming on CNBC about investing into savings accounts. Interest rates have been low for quite some time and it almost feels like you're losing money. I assure you that you're not. Preserving your cash is the utmost priority for emergency moments. A savings account, above all things, will ensure that.

Opening a savings account is easy. In fact, you've probably already done it at least once in your life. Walk into a bank or credit union and talk to a representative. Make sure you negotiate and understand the fees involved. If you are comfortable with banking online, there are plenty of providers available. You can find good high-yield accounts (savings and money market accounts) that are FDIC-insured. A few possibilities are:

- Ally Bank
- EverBank
- FNBO Direct
- Discover
- ING Direct

You can learn more about them at www.soldieroffinance.com/resources.

MIDDLE-DISTANCE HUMVEES:
INVESTMENT ACCOUNTS (INDIVIDUAL OR JOINT)

For traveling middle distances, you will need something that can carry you a little farther than your feet can handle. In the brokerage world, we call this an investment account. If you open the same type of account at a bank or credit union, it's more commonly known as a money market account or CD. This type of account should be used for goals that you'd want to accomplish in the next three to five years. This is an excellent place to accumulate money for things like a down payment on a home or your kids' braces fund. Because these things take a little more time, it's okay to tie up your money a little bit longer.

If you're risk averse, you'll want to stick to CDs. They are a safe way to get a reasonable return. The only drawback is that you have to leave the money in them for a few years. That is why they are not as good for emergency funds. They are not quite as easy to liquidate. What makes CDs less risky is the fact that they are normally FDIC-insured. The interest rates are a little lower, but if you worry a lot, CDs will help you sleep at night.

Depending on how much you dedicate to this pool of money, you might want to consider something called CD laddering. It is a way to protect you from locking in your money for too long. A CD ladder allows you to invest your money for different lengths of time ranging from six months to five years. Table 13-1 gives a quick example of what a $10,000 CD ladder divided equally over a five-year

Table 13-1 ▪ CD Ladder

$2,000 — 1-Year CD = 2.35%
$2,000 — 2-Year CD = 2.60%
$2,000 — 3-Year CD = 3.10%
$2,000 — 4-Year CD = 3.55%
$2,000 — 5-Year CD = 3.60%

period might look like.

Why use a CD ladder? Think of someone who is afraid of heights. It doesn't matter how much you pay him; he still will be afraid to climb to the top of a ladder. He might be okay climbing to the first or second rung, but any more than that and his heart starts to race and he is ready to jump off.

A CD ladder allows investors who are afraid of locking in their money for too long (the highest rung) to always have their feet on the first rung, maintaining a level of security, knowing that a CD will be maturing within the year. For example, assume that you are interested in opening a five-year CD to get the best rates, but you want to have access to some of the money yearly. A shorter-term CD does not provide a good APY (Annual Percentage Yield). Laddering allows you to benefit from the higher interest-earning potential and still have access to cash at regular intervals.

Open your five-year term CD with part of your funds, even if it is only the minimum required. That locks in the higher rate you wanted. Next, take the remaining amount of your investment money and open additional CD accounts with varying terms in increments of twelve months (one, two, three, and four years). The interest rate on those will be less than the five-year term. As each one-year CD comes due and you are sure you don't need the money, you can then lock up that CD at a five-year term knowing that you have another one coming due in a year.

PEER-TO-PEER LENDING

A new form of lending has appeared in recent years. If people need money to pay off a debt or start a business, and they can't get a traditional loan from a bank, they now have the option to use a peer-to-peer lending site. One of the biggest right now is called Lending Club (www.lendingclub.com).

You apply as you normally would for a loan and the organization completes a background check and a credit check, just as a bank would. Then it raises capital for the loan.

Raising the capital for the loan involves searching for investors willing to put up their money. For example, I might have $1,000 that I want to invest. I decide how much risk I want to take, and the Lending Club then selects the consumer note for me based on my tolerance level.

Typically, the risk is spread among numerous investors. If I have $1,000 invested, for example, only $25 will go to any one borrower, which further minimizes my risk. Instead of investing in corporate bonds, I'm investing directly in consumer loans. I've done this myself for several years now, and on average, I've made about 9% on my investments. With recent difficulties in the stock market, peer-to-peer lending has certainly gained traction.

Go / No Go

Short-Term and Middle-Distance Investments

Have you determined your basic goals? How long are you able, or willing, to leave money in an investment?

_____ **Go**   _____ **No Go**

Do you need quick access to your money?

_____ **Go**   _____ **No Go**

Have you compared the interest rates of savings accounts with money market accounts?

_____ **Go**   _____ **No Go**

SUMMARY

■ The type of investment vehicle you choose is determined by your goals. There are short-term investments as well as middle-distance and long-term vehicles.

■ Short-term investments should be as liquid as possible so that you have rapid access to them.

■ In the short term, a basic savings account allows you ready access to your funds and provides a safe, steady increase.

■ If you are comfortable with online banking, there are savings accounts that you can open that way.

■ Investment accounts provide better interest than do savings accounts. Commonly called money market accounts or CDs, they require a longer investment cycle.

■ Investment accounts are for goals that you want to accomplish in three to five years.

■ CD ladders give you more flexibility if you don't want to commit to a full five years.

■ Peer-to-peer lending provides an opportunity to lend money to private individuals through an organization that handles the loan details for you. The risk is spread among a number of private lenders.

WEEK 12

FIVE-TON TRUCKS AND MRAPs—LONG-DISTANCE INVESTMENT VEHICLES

As you learned in Chapter 13, when traveling on long convoys we relied on five-ton trucks to carry as many personnel as possible; my buddies in Afghanistan got to ride in MRAPs (Mine Resistant Ambush Protected vehicles). Both vehicles were built to transport big loads over long distances.

When it comes to investing for your retirement, you'll want to put your money in a vehicle designed to transport you into your golden years. You need to utilize retirement accounts engineered specifically for this purpose.

If you've joined the working force, the main vehicles you'll focus on will probably be Roth IRAs, traditional IRAs, and 401(k) plans. In essence, these vehicles enable you to invest in mutual funds, stocks, and bonds. As your investment portfolio grows, you might decide to buy specific stocks on your own. Long-term investments carry varying degrees of risk and varying yields. To effectively invest, you do not have to be an expert, but you do need to have enough understanding of how various vehicles work to choose the best for your situation and your temperament.

TAKE AN ACTIVE ROLE WITH A ROTH IRA

The first investment we will explore is the Roth IRA. If you have read other investment books, you already know that this advice is different from what is often recommended. Conventional wisdom says that if you can open a 401(k) with a good employer-matching plan, you should get your free money first and then look at other investment vehicles.

I don't agree with that advice. The reason is simple. As a Soldier of Finance, you must be actively involved in your investments, and you need to know what they are. Most people who sign up for a 401(k) get a form from their employer. They fill in some personal information, check a box or two regarding the types of investments they prefer, and hand it back. That's usually the last time they look at the account until they retire. They leave the 401(k) on autopilot and don't have a clue whether they're accessing the best investments or not.

I recommend a Roth IRA because it requires you to take action to open the account. You have to meet with a financial advisor or go online and physically do something; from the beginning you will be more engaged and more in control. Additionally, I'm a much bigger fan of tax-free money than free money, and when you eventually withdraw money from a Roth IRA it's tax-free.

Another factor is that 401(k) accounts usually have a limited number of options for investment. Even if you are paying attention to how your account is invested, you will probably only have a list of fifteen to twenty options at the most. A Roth IRA gives you many more choices.

Roth IRAs are limited in two ways. You must qualify, meaning that your modified adjusted gross income (MAGI) must be below a certain amount. If you are married and filing jointly, the limit is between $178,000 and $188,000. If you are single, the limit is between $112,000 and $127,000.

Note that if you make too much money to qualify for a Roth IRA, you can still open a traditional IRA. They operate much the same, except for how the money is taxed. The money in a Roth IRA is taxed before it goes into the account. A traditional IRA is taxed when you take the money out. Obviously, that makes the Roth IRA preferable, because all interest accrued is tax-free.

The second limitation is the total amount that you are allowed to deposit into the account. Basically, you can invest a maximum of $5,500, or $6,500 if you are over 50 years of age. For a married couple, the maximum is $11,000, or $13,000 if they are both over 50. Please note that the limits apply both to Roth and traditional IRAs. You are allowed to have both but you can only contribute the max between the two of them. These numbers are for 2013 and change every year, so check with the IRS to make sure you have the current limits.

One benefit of a Roth IRA is the ability to invest in a wide variety of options. The account itself is not a stock. Many people ask me, "How much does your IRA pay?" as though it generates interest on its own. In fact, it is an investment account into which you put money that is then invested in other vehicles. You don't buy an IRA, you open one. Then you buy investments with the account. How much interest you earn depends on what you buy.

You have a great deal of control over where you invest; you can choose from mutual funds or stocks or an ETF (exchange-traded fund) or CDs, among other options. The investment potential is much greater than it is with a 401(k).

Starting a Roth IRA account is no more complicated than filling out an application for a credit card or a bank account. You will need some basic information, including your Social Security number and bank account details. It can take as little as fifteen minutes and likely won't require more than an hour.

Deciding where to open your Roth IRA will take more effort than actually doing it. Your final decision depends on your comfort level. There are many options online, if you are comfortable with that. Fidelity Investments, Vanguard, and T. Rowe Price are three large companies to consider. Most banks and credit unions offer IRAs, though there could be limitations in what investments you can choose. You also can directly contact brokerage firms (I have worked with Scottrade). Other firms provide services as well; simply call their toll-free call center and speak with a rep. If you've never done this before, I recommend you meet with a financial advisor and discuss your options.

Before you make a decision, ask the following questions:

- Does the provider require a minimum initial investment?

- What fees are involved? Many funds have custodial fees, or fees that kick in if you don't hit a minimum amount of investment.

- What investment options are available?

- Is the provider reputable?

These questions are important. Banks might allow you to invest only in CDs. Scottrade has a huge mutual fund database, with thousands of possibilities to choose from, and does not require a minimum initial amount to open an account (although some of the funds in its database have minimum requirements). Some companies require minimum amounts to start; Fidelity requires $2,500 to open an account, though they will waive that if you commit to a $200 a month automatic contribution. You don't need much to get started, but if you don't have much, you will be more limited in your choices.

FOLLOW THE ROTH IRA WITH A 401(k)

While I prefer a Roth IRA to a 401(k), you should not ignore the 401(k) as a possible investment vehicle. There *are* advantages. You can invest much greater amounts than are allowed for Roth IRAs. The maximum annual amount allowed is currently $17,500, substantially more than the $5,500 for a Roth IRA. This number is also subject to change, so check with the IRS to be sure you are up-to-date.

Another advantage most 401(k) plans provide is an employer match program. Your employer might agree to match a portion of the money you put into the account, which is basically free money. If you have a 50 percent match, for example, your employer contributes 50 cents for every dollar you invest.

I advise my clients to start with a Roth IRA and max it out. Once they have reached the limit, they can consider starting a 401(k).

My apprehension about 401(k) accounts is that people rarely understand them or utilize them to their greatest benefit. Mechanically signing a form that their employer plugs into a default investment option, many people have no active participation in the process until they are ready to retire. The most important investment of their life, the money they will live on in retirement, is left in the hands of someone else. That's not the attitude of a Soldier of Finance. You should be in control of your financial decisions. Take responsibility.

The most common investment option allocated is the target-date mutual fund or a life-cycle fund. They are very similar. The idea is that the default fund your 401(k) investments are put into is determined by your age now compared with the date you expect to retire. Investments are designed to be more aggressive when you are young and become more conservative as you get closer to retirement. This sounds good in theory, but what often happens is that conglomerates of fifteen to twenty funds are thrown together. Breaking them down, I usually find at least one-quarter of them are bad choices.

On top of that, because funds are rebalanced periodically to fit your target date, you will have internal fees and end up paying up to twice as much as you would if you built your own portfolio. With target-date mutual funds, you normally end up with higher costs and lower return. Because most people leave the investment up to someone else, they never know how much they could be earning.

I once had four separate clients come in at the same time to review their 401(k) plans; all of them had used the default plan and all of them had target-date funds. My junior advisor and I went through them one at a time. The lowest interest rate was 2.5%, and the highest was just under 4%. Investigating alternate options, it became clear that leaving the funds as they were would result in losing out on tens of thousands of dollars in interest over a ten- to thirty-year period.

You do have a choice. Select a handful of good funds and refuse to use the others, lowering your expenses and eliminating funds that drag down your return. The options available for a 401(k) are limited, but look through them and choose the investments you want. Do not leave your fate in the hands of a default program that knows nothing about your personality or your goals.

A useful investment tool if you use it right, a 401(k) is not a savings account. You need to know how much you have in it and what it is invested into. At the same time, you need to let it work for you the way it is designed to work best. Many borrow against it and thereby defeat the purpose of building a retirement account. If you do that and lose your job, that money will have to be paid back or it will become taxed as a disbursement.

A 401(k) is not for day trading, either. You are likely to incur fees every time you make a change. Examine the available options, make decisions, and let the investment grow.

THE 401(k) FOR MILITARY PERSONNEL

If you're in the military or you have any other type of federal job, you will be offered a TSP (Thrift Savings Plan) rather than a 401(k). The TSP has the same flavor as a 401(k), but offers different investment options. Throughout my military career, I had the option of enrolling into a TSP, but decided against it. I felt the TSP's generic investment options did not allow me much control over the way my money would be invested.

THE STOCK MARKET: BE CAREFUL OF THE RISKS

Stocks are the single riskiest investment you can consider. If you have plenty of money that you won't miss if it all disappears, then stocks are for you. For most people, however, the risk isn't worth the gain.

If you do decide to develop a stock portfolio, remember that long-term stability is more important than making a quick buck. The stock market is usually something that people move into after they have built a substantial portfolio and have more money to work with. Stocks can make a lot of money very quickly, but they can also lose a lot just as fast.

I recommend staying away from stocks until you have enough extra money that you can invest without touching your core retirement investments. When you have extra money, and you don't mind the roller-coaster changes in the market, stocks can provide some dynamic investment opportunities.

The trick is in knowing which stocks to buy and when. There is no foolproof method for doing this. It's not enough to simply buy low and sell high. When you buy a stock, you are basically taking on a part ownership in that company. Good stock traders take the time to get to know the companies whose shares they buy.

The research involved is a subject far too complex to cover in detail. Because the stability of a company makes a great deal of difference in the outcome of your investment, it is wise to have some sort of familiarity with the company you're considering. For example, before I deployed to Iraq, I was aware of Under Armour sports clothing. My opinion was that it was overpriced, and I didn't pay much attention to it. But in Iraq, when it hit 140 degrees in the desert, I discovered why Under Armour used the slogan, "reflects the heat of the sun so you feel cooler and sweat less." It *was* more comfortable and it really did help to take moisture away from my body. I wore Under Armour underwear, Under Armour socks, and an Under Armour skullcap under my helmet. I could have been an Under Armour spokesperson. Sixty percent of our platoon wore the same brand. After that, I had no problem buying Under Armour stock. I completely believed in the company.

Price is not the only consideration. For long-term investments, consider the yield, that is, the dividend that the stock pays. Many stocks, such as AT&T, have been around for a long time and pay regular dividends. If you invest with the idea of building a regular flow of income from dividend profits, it won't matter how much the stock price fluctuates. As long as the company is stable, you'll have money coming in. It's kind of boring, but in the long term, it can provide significant passive income. If you are a conservative investor, leave the gambling to the day traders.

Stocks can give tremendous profits, but they also carry much greater risks than the other investment vehicles we have discussed. A Soldier of Finance weighs the risks involved and then acts accordingly.

DIVERSIFY BASED ON THE
SIZE OF YOUR PORTFOLIO

Most people have been told they should diversify, which means they should have a variety of investment vehicles in their portfolios. In other words, don't put all your eggs in one basket. If you invest everything in a single stock and it goes wrong, you will lose everything. Better advice would be to simply be aware of your situation and your opportunities. There is wisdom in spreading the risk around, but if you're just starting out, it seems a little silly to buy one share each of twenty different stocks. A young couple putting $50 a month into their investments doesn't need a lot of diversity. They need to build up some capital. For that kind of investor, I would likely recommend just two funds, a large stock company and an international stock fund. They might add a bond fund as their portfolio grows, adding a little stability.

Once you reach $10,000 in your accounts, diversity becomes more practical. Even then, you shouldn't just blindly diversify because some rule said you're supposed to. Steve Jobs wasn't diversified—he was Apple. Later he added Pixar. The risk is greater, but that doesn't mean you should automatically reject the possibility.

For most people, the amount of diversity needed depends on the size of the portfolio. Set some basic benchmarks. Start with a couple of investments until you have $10,000. Then add two or maybe three more. Once you hit $25,000, branch out a little more. The bigger your account, the more you have to lose, so do stay within your comfort range. Only you know how much risk you are willing to take.

INVESTING FOR YOUR FUTURE

The object is to accumulate a pool of money that allows you to retire comfortably and do the things you want to do. There are a multitude of investment opportunities, and unless you devote your full time to them, it's very difficult to keep up with all the options. These guidelines will give you a place to start, but ultimately, you will benefit by consulting an investment professional.

As we discussed in Chapter 12, you should not just sign with the first person you see. Check the advisor's track record. Make sure that person's investment philosophy matches yours. If he or she likes aggressive portfolios and you are more conservative, it might not be a good fit. Above all, take as much time as you can to educate yourself about various investment vehicles. The more you know, the better your decisions will be.

Go / No Go

Long-Term Investments

Does your employer offer a 401(k) plan?

_____ **Go**   _____ **No Go**

If you have a 401(k), do you know what funds it is invested in?

_____ **Go**   _____ **No Go**

Do you have a Roth IRA?

_____ **Go**   _____ **No Go**

Have you considered purchasing stock? If so, are you familiar with the company?

_____ **Go**   _____ **No Go**

SUMMARY

- The most common long-term investments are Roth IRAs, traditional IRAs, and 401(k) accounts.

- Long-term investments carry higher levels of risk, but generate greater profits.

- A Roth IRA is an ideal investment vehicle for people starting out. Many recommend starting with a 401(k), but there is a tendency to open the account and then ignore it, leaving the investments to be put into default funds and thereby limiting profits.

- A Roth IRA allows greater control over where the money is invested. It creates a more active involvement in the account, resulting in a greater awareness of details regarding the investment. It also allows the money to grow tax-free.

- The disadvantage of a Roth IRA is that there are limits on how much can be invested.

- The advantage of a 401(k) is that most accounts have a portion of your investment matched by your employer, basically giving you free money. There is also a much higher limit on how much can be invested.

- The disadvantage of a 401(k) is the limited selection for determining where your investments go. You have relatively little control.

- A traditional IRA is similar to a Roth IRA, except the money is taxed when you withdraw it.

- The stock market provides the greatest potential for profit but also the highest level of risk. Stock prices can fluctuate widely in a very short period of time. Investments in stocks should be limited to extra money that you can leave in the market for long periods of time.

- Stock purchases should be made after you familiarize yourself with the company that issues the stock. You should know something about the company and believe in its product before you invest.

- Most people say that you should diversify your portfolio. However, if you have relatively little invested, too much diversity is an unnecessary complication. The larger your portfolio, the greater the need for diversity to reduce the risks of losing it all.

PART FOUR

CONSOLIDATION PHASE (WEEKS 13–14)

Phase Three is designed to consolidate and expand your initial campaign. The attack has been launched. In order to organize and expand the territory taken during your financial campaign, it is necessary to understand the basics of real estate and insurance.

By the end of the Consolidation Phase, you will be well on your way to completing some of your short-term goals and you will have a clear vision of your lifetime goals and how to accomplish them.

WEEK 13

BASIC HOUSING
ALLOWANCE—
MORTGAGE BASICS

War is a terrible thing. The first time you see a human being wounded and bleeding, it leaves a lasting impression. You understand it is serious business. Why would anyone subject himself to the pressures and risks synonymous with combat? I don't know that I ever thought about that question at the time. Looking back, I realize the answer would have been different at different periods in my life.

When I enlisted, my real goal was to get the government to pay for my college education. There was some nebulous concept of fighting for home and country, but most of us who enlisted never really thought we would have to fight. Not for real.

In combat, you do have that sense of fighting for the folks back home, but the truth is, most soldiers fight for other reasons. The camaraderie that builds between brothers in arms is most important. You fight because you don't want to let your Battle Buddies down. You learn to depend on each other, and nothing else matters.

Of course, if you asked us, we would maintain that we fought to defend the American Dream. The only thing is, we often weren't sure what that meant. The phrase is vaguely associated with equality and the opportunity to achieve in life according to your ability. Life, liberty, and the pursuit of happiness are part of the American Dream. Happiness and stability for your family might be the general idea. I believe that most people pursue this fuzzy dream without really thinking too deeply about it. Yet, when asked to describe it, most people include a house as part of their vision. Owning your own home is essentially inseparable from the American Dream. You know you are a success when you buy a house.

The reality of that dream became evident with the collapse of the real estate market in 2008. The ease with which people could obtain mortgage loans meant that many thousands of people purchased houses they could not afford. Eventually, the difficulty of keeping up with payments and maintenance expenses beyond their income caught up with them and foreclosures skyrocketed. The American Dream became a nightmare for many.

My mom is a good example of what happened to a large number of people. At the peak of the market she sold her home in Los Angeles and decided to move to Las Vegas, where she was able to pay cash for her retirement home.

Had she left it at that, she'd have been set for life. However, she wanted to invest in real estate. At the time, real estate prices were steadily rising and many were making a fortune flipping houses.

The story did not turn out that way for my mom. She had declared bankruptcy within the previous seven years, so her credit was not good. I refused to cosign for her, but that being the heyday of

Freddie Mac and Fannie Mae, when almost anyone could get a mortgage, she managed to use the surplus cash from the sale of her LA home as a down payment on three investment properties.

Unfortunately, when the housing bubble burst, she was unable to sustain the investments. All three properties dropped to 30 percent of their purchase price and she was unable to find either buyers or renters, which eventually forced her to short-sell all of them. Like many others, she didn't think through the details of property purchases and she lost heavily. The fact that most of the nation shared her experience didn't make it any more pleasant.

Reflecting on the American Dream, I've come to realize that the most important thing you fight for is the relationships you have built. Your family's well-being and financial security are far more important than the place where you live. If you can afford a house, that's great. If you can't, it doesn't mean you never will be able to. It's a worthy goal, but you must approach it with the same deliberate planning and common sense you would any other mission. It's only a worthwhile goal if it doesn't cripple your finances and leave you struggling to pay for it.

DEBRIEFING

J. Money's House

Personal finance blogger J. Money, of www.BudgetsAreSexy.com, shared some of his experience and opinions with me. Offering insights that run a little contrary to the usual advice you are likely to hear about the American Dream, his story asks some important questions. In spite of the fact that he regularly blogs on finance issues, he made the same mistakes as most people. He jumped into a house purchase without thinking it through very well:

"I wasn't in debt or in any financial trouble at all, but I also wasn't saving a lot, nor did I have much of an idea of where I wanted to be fi-

nancially (besides 'wanting to be a millionaire,' as we all do). And the same went with my career. I had recently been promoted a few times within the start-up company I was working for, but other than that I was humming along regularly without much thought of what I actually wanted to DO with my life. I was playing by the rules as most other Americans do, and when the idea to buy a house came up we figured 'why not?'."

Like most Americans, there was no thought of running the numbers or really considering how difficult the responsibility of owning a house would be.

"We talked with the financial department of the realtor we were using at the time, and we knew we were somewhat financially sound, but we never really played with the numbers much or had a REAL budget at the time. Unless you count the 'fake' ones in our heads that most of us have. It literally came down to them saying, 'You can afford X amount' and us using that as a gauging point. Which makes me shudder just thinking about it."

With that they started looking, found a house they loved, and closed the deal. They literally took a wrong turn and came across their "dream house."

"It was such a nice place on a gorgeous lake that all we could think back then was, 'WOW! If only we could afford this!' And forty-eight hours later we were putting in a contract."

The story had a good ending, but not without problems that could have been avoided. I asked J. Money at what point he realized that living the American Dream wasn't all it was cracked up to be.

"When I realized that I would have to keep working my a$$ off in order to live this lifestyle we created for ourselves at that moment. Going from a one-bedroom apartment to an entire townhouse with three levels made me realize over time that (a) we didn't need all of that room, but even more so (b) that now we were forced to continue earning X amount in order to keep up with the house and everything else that came with it (maintenance, homeowner fees, insurance, etc.).

(Continues on next page)

And after deciding to be more minimalistic than I had been my entire year before that point, it irked me even more.

I now had to pay a ton more money just to keep things going! And not only that, but due to the market crashing all around us at the exact same time we bought, we weren't free to just 'get up and go' anytime we wanted anymore. Which really struck me hard. Yeah, it sucked our house was losing value when everyone said it was a 'great investment,' but more so was the feeling of being stuck. It was a hard pill to swallow having lived a military lifestyle my whole life, and it made it worse knowing I brought it all on myself! Because I didn't think and just figured it would all work itself out because everyone knows buying a home is the American Dream. HAH! It may be for most of society, but it's definitely not for everyone. And I was a dummy for falling for it."

HOW MUCH HOUSE CAN YOU REALLY AFFORD?

The great thing about the American Dream is that anyone can grow into it. The single biggest investment that most Americans will ever make is their home. You want to make sure it's a sound investment and that you can actually afford it.

Keep in mind that banks make their profits by lending money and charging interest. In the current economic climate, in which we have regularly seen guaranteed mortgages and bank bailouts, banks have no real incentive to manage their risk. The more they can get you to borrow, the more money they will make. If you default, the government will take care of their losses. The one who loses will be you.

With that in mind, approach qualifying for a loan with some caution. Since the collapse of the housing market, loans are much more difficult to get, but that doesn't mean you should trust the numbers the bank gives you. If they tell you that you qualify for a $500,000 loan, that doesn't mean you have to use all of it, or that you should use all of it. That number means nothing more than what it says. The bank will give you that much.

What usually happens is that buyers see the amount they qualify for and immediately start looking at homes in that price range. Before you go that route, take the time to run your own numbers.

Bank calculations are based roughly on a comparison of the price of the house with your total income. That's the same thing you should do. As a general rule, when you compare the median home prices to your income, it should be a ratio of three or below. That means that if your combined household income is $100,000, you should look at houses less than three times that amount, under $300,000.

Another way to calculate how much home you can afford is to calculate the ratio of your income to the expenses involved in owning the house. Taxes can vary considerably from place to place, so use your net income for this calculation. According to this method, you should spend no more than one-third of your net income on total housing costs. These costs include:

- Mortgage payment

- Property taxes

- Insurance

- Electricity

- Fees (such as homeowners association)

- Maintenance costs

If the monthly expenses are greater than a third of your net monthly income, you will struggle to keep up with the cost of your house. *Do not trust the bank alone to tell you how much house you qualify for. Work your own numbers.*

WHAT TYPES OF LOANS ARE BEST FOR YOU?

Mortgages are secured loans using your house as collateral. The loans can be structured as fixed rate mortgages, adjustable rate mortgages, and a variety of hybrid loans that combine features of both. Here is a brief look at each type:

- **Fixed Rate Mortgages.** The term "fixed rate" means that you lock in the interest rate for the entire duration of the loan. Typically these loans are for thirty or fifteen years, though they can be for as little as ten and as many as forty.

  With fixed rate loans, you gradually pay down the principal. In the early years, most of the payment is interest. The longer the loan goes, the greater the percentage of payment that is applied to the principal. Most fixed rate mortgages allow you to make additional payments on the principal at any time, reducing the total loan and saving on interest down the road.

  One disadvantage of a fixed rate loan is that if interest rates drop five years from the time you bought your house, you are stuck with the higher rate. The advantage is that you know the rate will not increase.

- **Variable Rate Mortgages.** As suggested by the name, a variable rate mortgage has an interest rate that fluctuates over the duration of the loan. A variety of indexes affect the rate changes, such as the Certificate of Deposit Index and the prime rate. Most adjustable rate mortgages have caps to protect you from enormous increases, but when the interest rates go up, so does your monthly payment. The advantage is, if rates drop, you will likely be rewarded with a lower payment.

- **Hybrid Mortgages.** A wide variety of options are available through creative financing. Usually this results in monthly payments that increase over time. For example, it is possible to have a very low payment for five years, followed by rapidly increasing payments for a few years.

Which type of mortgage you use depends on several factors, including the amount you can afford for payments and how long you expect to stay in the house. If you plan to be in a house for just a few years, and then sell it and move to another location, a graduated payment might be a good option. This is where the initial loan payment starts low and gradually increases over a specified time frame until it reaches the full payment level. If you plan to stay for a long time, ten years or more, a fixed rate will usually be better in the long run. If the interest rates are high when you purchase, a variable rate mortgage would be a good choice, although there is no way to predict what future rates will be.

Real estate is a complex decision; take plenty of time to consider all the factors involved. I can only offer a basic guideline.

HOUSING TRAPS TO AVOID

There is a lot to think about when buying a house. Here are four important points that are often overlooked:

1. **Don't take anyone's advice about what you can afford.** Your agent is paid by commission on the sale and so has no reason to care whether or not you can afford the house. And if the loan is guaranteed by the government, the bank won't care if you default on it. The more house the bank gets you to buy, the more money it will make. Do not take anyone's advice except your own. Take an honest look at your income and debt load as well as the price of the house and the expenses associated with it, and then decide what you can afford. Does the house need repairs? Take that into consideration. If it's an old house, it will probably need a lot more work. Is the house in a downtown area? Consider what your

property taxes will be. Take the time to consider e*verything*. You will have a lot of money tied up, so don't be rushed into anything.

2. **Investigate the neighborhood.** Begin by simply driving around and seeing what's nearby. How close are schools? Do you want that many kids wandering by your property every day? What is traffic like at different times of day? Are you close to fire stations? That can be good for your insurance costs, but it will also mean hearing sirens at all hours.

   Take the time to visit some of the neighbors. Ask them what they like about the neighborhood and what they don't like. Perhaps there's a crazy person who lives on the corner, or half the neighbors hate the other half and have an ongoing feud that you don't want to be part of. Ideally, you may learn that the neighbors are all friendly and watch out for each other. Investigate zoning for surrounding empty properties; you don't want to move in and then discover that a mall is starting construction a block away. Educate yourself thoroughly about what you're getting into.

3. **Don't open and close credit accounts.** Every time you start or close a credit line, it dings your credit score. A few changes like this can drop your score as much as 30 points, sabotaging your mortgage interest rate when you most need your score to be at its highest.

4. **Don't buy until you're ready.** As I pointed out at the beginning of this chapter, the American Dream is not owning a home at any cost; the American Dream is living a life of security and fulfillment with your family. If buying a house undermines your financial security, you don't have to do it right away.

For that matter, you don't have to do it at all. J. Money's experience should be a lesson. Ultimately he enjoyed his house, but when

I asked him what advice he would give to young people considering buying their first home, he made the following pointed comment:

"Really, REALLY, make sure you understand all the pros and cons about owning a home. Even if you can afford it (or someone says you can afford it), make sure you genuinely want to own a home and have solid reasons for it. It's not always an 'investment' or the 'smartest way to live,' because we all want different things out of our lives."

The bottom line is this: The fact that everyone says homeownership is a big part of the American Dream doesn't mean it has to be *your* dream. It's a great goal to strive for, but make sure you've done the groundwork first. Take the time to do your homework so that when you do buy, it will be an experience to remember and not one that you rather forget.

Go / No Go

Buying a House

Have you determined how much you can afford to spend on a house, given your current income?

_____ Go   _____ No Go

Do you really need a house right now? Can you afford it? Or should you deal with debt first?

_____ Go   _____ No Go

Have long do you plan to live in the house?

_____ Go   _____ No Go

(Continues on next page)

What type of mortgage best suits your goals?

_____ Go   _____ No Go

SUMMARY

- Owning a house is part of the American Dream, but it might not be the best financial move for you at this point in your life. That doesn't mean you will never own one, but your family's financial security is more important than where you live. If your dream is a house, you must approach it with deliberate planning and common sense.

- Be realistic about how much house you can afford. Just because the bank says you can have a mortgage for a specific amount doesn't mean you have to use all of it.

- As a general rule, when you compare median home prices to your income, the ideal is a ratio of three or below.

- There are different types of loans: Fixed rate mortgages lock in the interest rate for the duration of the loan. Variable rate mortgages offer fluctuating interest rates over the duration of the loan. A hybrid mortgage combines a variety of options. Which type is best for you depends on your income, situation, and goals.

- When buying a house, don't take anyone else's advice about how much you can afford. Investigate the neighborhood. Do not open and close credit accounts prior to applying for the mortgage, because doing so will lower your credit score. And don't buy until you are ready.

WEEK 14

YOUR BODY ARMOR— YOU NEED INSURANCE

Soldiers in the field with their helmets and gear always looked bulky to me. I discovered that the reason behind this was extra body armor. More than a bulletproof vest, it covers the entire upper body. Body armor is standard issue for all military personnel in war zones like Iraq and Afghanistan.

When I was issued an IBA (Interceptor Body Armor), otherwise known as a flak jacket, my knees and lower back started aching as soon as I picked it up. My initial reaction was that I now had an extra sixteen pounds to carry around with all my other gear. I wasn't happy about it.

Of course, body armor has a purpose. It stops projectiles from penetrating your skin; it protects you. You can go into combat with or without it, but given the choice, *with* makes a lot more sense. Your chances of sustaining a fatal injury are greatly reduced. The entire time I was in Iraq, I hated it. It was hot, heavy, and annoying. But I wore it. I saw many lives saved because soldiers had that protection.

I view insurance in much the same way: as protection. It provides the means to take care of specific emergencies that you cannot afford on your own. Above all, insurance protects your family if anything happens to you.

More than 35 million American households have no life insurance, and that number is growing. This represents a 22 percent increase in just the past six years. The economy is largely at fault, but the end result is that one-third of Americans have no life insurance to cover their family's expenses if they die.

Fewer Americans now have homeowners or renters insurance. A surprising number of people also don't have auto insurance, even though it is legally required in most states.

I don't spend a lot of my time getting people into insurance programs, but I do recognize that a certain amount of insurance is absolutely vital. You need to protect yourself in some key areas. Specifically, there are five types of insurance you absolutely must have:

1. Auto insurance

2. Homeowners/renters insurance

3. Medical insurance

4. Life insurance

5. Umbrella liability

The following gives a basic overview of each. As with any type of investment, you should ask plenty of questions and learn all you can before making a decision.

AUTO INSURANCE

The most obvious insurance coverage required is auto. It is "obvious" because, in most states, legally, you have to have it. A few considerations, however, could save you a lot of money.

First and foremost is liability. If you are in an accident and anyone is injured, medical expenses can be overwhelming. Make sure you have that covered. In many cases the law requires it, but you cannot afford to ignore it even if it is not legally required.

The amount of coverage you buy depends on your car and how stable your FRAGO Fund is. If you drive an older car that can be replaced for a few thousand dollars, and you have that money in your emergency fund, you might consider dropping collision coverage and saving on the premiums. It is a gamble, but if you have an excellent driving record, it could be worth considering. If you have a poor record, however, or if the replacement value of your car is more than you could take care of without undue hardship, be sure your insurance protects you from accidents.

Shopping around is a good way to find the lowest prices on anything, but know what you're getting. Some companies "save" you money by providing less coverage. Examine the insurance package closely and be sure it includes exactly what you need.

A quick way to save money on premiums is to keep deductibles high. Increasing the deductible from $200 to $500 can save as much as 30 percent on the premium. Of course, if you are in an accident, you will have to pay the deductible. If you have an emergency fund set up, which you should by now, you can self-insure against smaller damages and use the insurance to protect you from major losses.

Ask about discounts. Many insurance companies offer a variety of discounts for specific conditions: Teen drivers can be offered discounts for good grades or participation in certain driver's education programs. If you work close to home and don't drive much, ask if you're eligible for a low-mileage deduction. Some companies offer lower deductibles for each year that passes without a claim. It never hurts to ask a lot of questions. Who knows what you will learn?

Before buying a new vehicle, discuss it with your insurance agent; some cars cost less to insure than others.

HOMEOWNERS/RENTERS INSURANCE

If you experience a disaster such as a fire or flood, you want to know that your home and possessions can be replaced. This is true whether you own the home or are renting. Belongings often have great personal and sentimental value, which can never be replaced, but if you experience disaster it will be comforting to know that you'll be able to buy clothes and the necessities for living that we often take for granted.

You can choose either a cash value policy or a replacement cost policy. Cash value pays you the value of the home at the time it was destroyed. A replacement cost policy is more expensive, but it covers whatever rebuilding costs you encounter in bringing the new home to the same quality as the old one. Once you have a homeowners policy, inform your agent of any improvements made on the house. Many homes are underinsured because owners neglect to upgrade the policy following major additions to the home.

One common error is to insure both the house and the land on which it sits for replacement costs in case of a disaster. You won't have to replace the land; you only need to insure the house. This oversight increases premium costs and gives you nothing in return.

Possessions need to be covered. If you are renting, this is the purpose of renters insurance. Valuable items such as jewelry, antiques, or art pieces (paintings, statues, sculptures) often require a specific rider on the policy. Be sure you inquire.

Typically possessions are covered up to 75 percent of their face value. It is important to maintain an inventory of your possessions and keep it at another location. You wouldn't want the inventory list to be destroyed along with the rest of the house. Videotaping your home is an easy way to maintain a record. You can keep recordings and pictures of your home in a safe, or you can videotape a walk-through of your home and upload it to YouTube (using privacy settings, of course, so that no one can view it). That way, a record is available to you no matter what happens to your home. Failure to keep a written or video inventory current could result in only being able to claim a fraction of the value of your possessions if they are stolen or damaged.

As is the case with auto insurance, increasing your deductible will decrease your premiums. In addition, many companies offer loyalty discounts if you stay with them for the long haul. You may also get a discount if you insure your home and auto with the same company. Improving your home's security and disaster resistance often results in further reduction of the premiums. An agent who wants your business will gladly answer your questions. Be sure to ask plenty.

MEDICAL INSURANCE

If you are still working, your most important asset is your career. Your ability to earn a living is something that you cannot do without. Medical insurance is far more likely to be used than is life insurance. Your medical insurance needs to cover any disability that interrupts your income. Hospitalization is extremely expensive, as is long-term nursing care if you become disabled.

Most people have medical insurance, to some extent, through their employer. If you do not, explore your options; while expensive, it is vital in the long run. Take a close look at the policy—even if your employer covers you—to check for gaps in coverage that can be covered with a personal policy.

Many people simply can't afford private medical insurance. However, something is better than nothing, so explore alternate options. Many states now offer basic health insurance based on income levels. Call your state offices for more information. As with most types of insurance, raising your deductible will lower the premium. Take the time to compare plans to get the best possible coverage that you can afford. Take advantage of a health savings account, which allows you to put aside money to pay for medical expenses, tax-free.

When I first started my business, we were covered by insurance with my wife's employer. However, when she decided to quit that job, we needed private insurance. Using www.eHealthinsurance.com as a source, we spoke to several local agents. After taking reams of notes, and spending what felt like days on the phone, asking lots of questions, we finally found what we were looking for.

The lesson from our experience is that you can find a workable policy if you persevere. When you consider the impact a serious illness requiring hospitalization could have on your financial future, it is worth the effort to make sure you are covered.

LIFE INSURANCE

There is an old *Wizard of Id* cartoon in which a life insurance salesman pitches his product to the king. The king asks him, "What's life insurance?"

The salesman responds, "That's where we bet that you will give us more money before you die than we have to give you in return."

The king asks, "What if I die young?"

"Then you win."

Perhaps a rather cynical approach, it does highlight the essential element behind life insurance. Its purpose is to take care of people after you die.

A few years ago, a recent widow sat in my office, clenching a box of tissues and sharing her story with me. She and her husband had been together for over twenty years; they had two kids and loved each other deeply. He was a hard worker, very health conscious, and took great care of himself. It was a devastating shock when she walked into the kitchen and found the love of her life lying lifeless on the floor.

He had taken the time to provide for his family, however, by taking out a very large life insurance policy. He was the primary breadwinner for the family, so if he hadn't bought insurance, the sudden loss of his income would have left his wife and children destitute. Due to her husband's foresight, the woman never had to work again and the kids were able to continue on to college. The loss of a close family member is tough enough without having to worry about money. "Had he not bought that [life insurance]," she told me, "I have no idea what I would have done."

Unfortunately, according to a recent survey, more than 35 million U.S. households have no life insurance. Yet the one thing you can be sure of is that you are 100 percent guaranteed to die. Provision for your family is important after you are gone.

Many don't buy life insurance because they believe they can't afford it. The truth is that a healthy 35-year-old man can get $500,000 of term insurance for 20 years for the price of six Double-Doubles per month at In-N-Out Burger. The policy won't taste as good as a Double-Double, but you can rest assured that your family is taken care of. And cutting back on burgers might help you to live longer.

I'm not a huge proponent of insurance as an investment tool. Those varieties include whole life, universal, variable, and indexed. Some are useful for transferring money to your children without incurring heavy tax burdens, so I won't say you should never use permanent insurance, but I do not believe that it is the best investment for most people. The purpose of insurance is to provide death benefits. The cheapest way you can arrange that is usually the best kind of insurance to use. If you live, that's good. If you die and your spouse eventually dies, your descendants benefit. So you do win either way.

Term insurance is literally pennies on the dollar compared to whole life. A policy for $250,000 could be as little as $20 a month. That means a quarter of a million dollars in life insurance could be paid for by the price of two movie tickets every month. That's a pretty good return on your money, should your family need it.

Instead of paying hundreds of dollars each month for something that will only generate face value if you die, why not spend $20 a month for term insurance and put the balance into a more profitable investment? If you use it to start a Roth IRA, you will be light years ahead by the time you retire.

I took out a policy when I got married and another when we had our first child. If you are single, it's not as important because you have only yourself to worry about. But if you have a spouse or children, you need to protect them. How much life insurance you should have depends on several factors:

■ What kind of lifestyle do you want for your family after you are gone?

■ Does your spouse work, and will he/she be able to continue working?

■ How much debt do you have?

■ What will be your family's insurance needs, especially medical?

- What will be required for your family to keep their house?

- Do you want insurance that will provide a lump sum to cover these expenses or do you want to set up a regular income for them?

The answers to those questions will help you get an idea of how much life insurance you need. Consider the answers and go shopping. The tricky thing about insurance is that you are guessing at what might happen in the future, and those projections are likely to change as time goes by. Getting the amount exactly right isn't the issue; providing protection for your family's security is. Once you have a decent estimate, go with it. You can reevaluate your circumstances every few years and adjust accordingly.

Periodically reviewing your coverage and premium amount is important for the same reason as refinancing your mortgage loan: You may find better rates and be able to renegotiate the policy. I recently used a life insurance quote engine to see how much money I could save if I refinanced. I was surprised to learn I could get $250,000 more coverage for $400 per year less. That's a savings of $12,000 over a period of thirty years! If I invested that into something that paid 7% each year, I would end up much further ahead.

There is one important point to consider if you change your policies: You don't want to lose any coverage during the process. For this reason, *do not cancel your existing policy until you are approved for the new one.* It would be very unfortunate to let one policy lapse and then experience a medical condition that prevented you from either getting the new policy or renewing the old one. In my case, I made the regular premium payment on the policy I already had while awaiting approval for the new one. After the change to the new policy was complete, I canceled the old one and got a refund for a pro-rated amount of the premium I had paid.

UMBRELLA LIABILITY: COVERING THE GAPS

An umbrella policy basically rests on your existing insurance policies for your vehicles and home, providing extra protection in the event of a situation not fully covered by your normal insurance. Umbrella policies cover the gaps left by other coverage. For example, if a friend trips over a garden hose in your yard and sues you for negligence, your umbrella policy would cover you.

All kinds of liabilities can be covered. They are often things that you would not normally think about, but for which you can incur considerable legal responsibility. A few examples demonstrate how important this coverage is:

- **Scenario 1:** Suppose you throw a party at your home, serving alcohol, and a minor has a few drinks without your knowing about it. Then he drives home and gets in a wreck. Even though you were not aware of the problem until later, you could be held legally liable for damage or injuries.

- **Scenario 2:** Perhaps you act as a chaperone for several kids on a field trip to the park and one of them is injured. Even though it was something you could never have foreseen, the parents of the injured child might claim you were intentionally negligent because your kid didn't like their kid. So they sue you for damages.

- **Scenario 3:** While driving home you accidentally collide with a delivery truck hauling very expensive equipment.

- **Scenario 4:** Your child borrows a friend's car to run to the store. On the way back, he runs a stop sign and smashes into a mini-van that's carrying a family of four.

You could find yourself in court over any of these incidents. Considering how litigious our culture is, you must protect yourself with the right umbrella policy. These policies usually come in $1 million increments, and I recommend a $1 million policy as a minimum.

As with many financial matters, don't trust the judgment of a salesman. Do your own calculations. Salesmen all have a formula that they apply to everyone; you are an individual with a unique life. Take the time to figure out your own needs. The issue is protection of all the efforts you have put into your financial future.

Go / No Go

Insurance Needs

Have you shopped around for the least expensive auto insurance?

_____ **Go**   _____ **No Go**

Do you have an inventory list of your possessions stored in a safe place?

_____ **Go**   _____ **No Go**

Do you have medical insurance available through an employer?

_____ **Go**   _____ **No Go**

How much money would your family need if you died? Do you have sufficient life insurance to cover that possibility?

_____ **Go**   _____ **No Go**

SUMMARY

- Insurance is protection against unexpected emergencies beyond what your FRAGO Fund covers.

- There are five types of insurance you cannot do without: auto, homeowners/renters, medical, life, and umbrella liability.

- Auto insurance is required in most states. At the very least you need to have liability. Premiums can be lowered by raising your deductible, as well as by taking advantage of other discounts. Be sure to ask about them.

- Homeowners/renters insurance provides replacement for possessions lost due to disaster or theft. You can choose cash value or a replacement cost policy. Keep up-to-date records of all your possessions stored somewhere other than your home.

- Medical insurance is necessary to cover sickness or injury that might threaten your ability to work. As with other types of insurance, raising your deductible can lower premiums.

- The purpose of life insurance is to provide for your family if you die. Term life insurance is affordable for most people. Insurance policies designed to be an investment are rarely the best investment vehicle available to you.

- Umbrella policies cover a wide variety of liabilities for fluke accidents.

CONCLUSION

At the beginning of your training here, you completed the Go/No Go: Performance Measure. That initial evaluation gave you a snapshot of your financial life and habits. Now that you are at the end of this book, it's time to see how far you've come. Go back to Chapter 1, complete the Performance Measure evaluation again, and compare the results to the first one. I think you'll be pleased.

You are now a Soldier of Finance. You have developed key skills, and you have planned missions and achieved objectives. But this doesn't mean your training is finished. Being a Soldier of Finance is not a course of training that you complete and then leave behind once you pass a test. It is a new beginning. The oath you took was for the rest of your life. Maintaining success requires follow-through in pursuing your lifetime goals as vigorously as you pursued and accomplished your short-term objectives.

Recently I was asked the difference between being a soldier and being a civilian. The distinctive characteristics of a member of the U.S. Army are the same for a Soldier of Finance:

- **Discipline:** A Soldier of Finance continues to vigilantly follow his code of conduct for financial success. He is consistent and reliable. He is dependable.

- **Clear Vision:** A Soldier of Finance is focused, striving to define the bigger picture and pursue his goals with singleness of purpose.

- **Tested:** A Soldier of Finance has put the principles of money to work and has tested them. He has seen that they work because he has persistently followed them. He has overcome obstacles to his success.

- **Knowledge:** A Soldier of Finance has an understanding of the tools and weapons available to him for waging his campaign. He has taken the time to learn how to use them and he has applied them to his financial life.

- **Confidence:** A Soldier of Finance stands with the confidence that comes from training, experience, and comradeship with his Battle Buddies.

In short, a Soldier of Finance has achieved more than just learning a few steps to attain an outcome. He has learned to think, analyze, and plan his life, giving him the confidence to live it with boldness and strength.

Perhaps you think I've overstated the case, but you have to admit, now that you have a grip on your financial life, you do feel a lot better about the future. That's what really counts. Now that you have eliminated your No Go's and replaced them with Go's, the time has come to Go and Conquer.

RESOURCES

For a more in-depth review of all the resources below, go to www
.soldieroffinance.com/resources.

Jeff's Other Sites

- www.goodfinancialcents.com
- www.debtmovement.com
- www.lifeinsurancebyjeff.com

Free Credit Report

- www.annualcreditreport.com

Free Credit Score

- True Fico Score: www.myfico.com

Consumer Education Credit Scores

- www.credit.com
- www.quizzle.com
- www.creditkarma.com

Online Savings

- www.ally.com

- www.capitalone.com

Online Brokerages

- www.scottrade.com

- www.betterment.com

- www.etrade.com

Find a Financial Advisor

- www.napfa.org

- www.cfp.net

Free Life Insurance Quote

- www.lifeinsurancebyjeff.com

INDEX

ABOUT THE AUTHOR

Jeff Rose is a Certified Financial Planner™ professional who has founded his own investment advisory firm, Alliance Wealth Management, LLC. He is the founder and chief editor of GoodFinancial Cents.com, a top 20 personal finance blog according to Wise bread.com.

Jeff is also the mastermind behind The Debt Movement—the goal of which is to help people pay off $10 million of debt. You can follow their progress at DebtMovement.com.

He currently writes for *U.S. News and World Report* (www.US News.com), Equifax, and *Market Watch* (owned by the *Wall Street Journal*). He has been featured in major media sites such as Huffington Post, Forbes, Reuters, Kiplingers, and Fox Business.

A nine-year veteran of the Army National Guard, his unit was called up in January 2005 to support Operation Iraqi Freedom. Acquiring the rank Staff Sergeant, he served as Squad Leader while conducting military police maneuvers in central Baghdad. He returned home safely to his beautiful wife, Mandy, in April 2006.

When he's not corralling his three boys, Parker, Bentley, and Sloane, you'll find him on the floor of his local Crossfit box gasping from another torturous WOD (workout of the day).

Besides Crossfitting, his passions include blogging, spending time with his family, cheering on the St. Louis Cardinals, or fantasizing about the next time he can sink his teeth into an In-N-Out Burger.

May I never boast except in the cross of our Lord Jesus Christ,
through which the world has been crucified to me, and I to the world.
—GALATIANS 6:14

CPSIA information can be obtained
at www.ICGtesting.com
Printed in the USA
LVHW032253270219
609002LV00008B/132/P